PENGUIN BO

LEARNING TO PHILOSOPHIZE

E. R. Emmet was born in 1909 and was educated at Rossall and at Brasenose College, Oxford. After taking Honour Moderations in Mathematics he spent his last two years at Oxford reading Philosophy, Politics and Economics. Since 1932, except for a break of two years for writing, he has been teaching mathematics, economics and philosophy at Winchester, where he was a housemaster from 1947 to 1963.

He has contributed to philosophical journals and is the author of *An Introduction to Economics* (with R. C. Lyness), *The Use of Reason*, *Learning to Think*, *101 Brain-Puzzlers*, *Puzzles for Pleasure* (published in the U.S.A.), *The Puffin Book of Brainteasers* and *A Diversity of Puzzles*.

E. R. Emmet died in March 1980.

LEARNING
TO PHILOSOPHIZE

E. R. EMMET

PENGUIN BOOKS

PENGUIN BOOKS

Published by the Penguin Group
Penguin Books Ltd, 27 Wrights Lane, London W8 5TZ, England
Viking Penguin, a division of Penguin Books USA Inc.
375 Hudson Street, New York, New York 10014, USA
Penguin Books Australia Ltd, Ringwood, Victoria, Australia
Penguin Books Canada Ltd, 2801 John Street, Markham, Ontario, Canada L3R 1B4
Penguin Books (NZ) Ltd, 182–190 Wairau Road, Auckland 10, New Zealand

Penguin Books Ltd, Registered Offices: Harmondsworth, Middlesex, England

First published by Longmans 1964
This revised edition published in Pelican Books 1968
Reprinted in Penguin Books 1991
1 3 5 7 9 10 8 6 4 2

Printed in England by Clays Ltd, St Ives plc
Set in Monotype Plantin

TO MY WIFE

CONTENTS

ACKNOWLEDGEMENTS

We are indebted to the following for permission to reproduce copyright material:

Basil Blackwell and the executors of the Wittgenstein Estate for material from Wittgenstein: *Philosophical Investigations*, trans. G. E. M. Anscombe; The Bodley Head Ltd for material from *Principia Ethica* by G. E. Moore; Cambridge University Press and The Macmillan Company for material from *Adventures by Ideas* by A. N. Whitehead; the author's agents and Phoenix House Publications for material from *The Power of Words* by Stuart Chase; The Clarendon Press for material from *Sense and Sensibilia* by J. L. Austin, *Some Problems in Ethics* by H. W. B. Joseph and *Doubt and Certainty in Science* by J. Z. Young; the author and Macmillan & Co. Ltd for material from *The Case for Modern Man* by Charles Frankel; The Hutchinson Publishing Group for material from *The Concept of Mind* by Gilbert Ryle; Kant-Studien for material from *Value Theory as a Formal System* by R. S. Hartman; Macmillan & Co. Ltd for material from *Creative Evolution* by Henri Bergson; Manchester University Press for material from *Discourse on Metaphysics* by G. W. Leibniz, trans. P. G. Lucas and L. Grint; the author's agents and Doubleday & Company, Inc. for material from *A Writer's Notebook* by W. Somerset Maugham, copyright 1949 by W. Somerset Maugham; Methuen & Co. Ltd for material from *The Theory of Beauty* by E. F. Carritt; Oxford University Press for material from *The Problems of Philosophy* by Bertrand Russell; Routledge & Kegan Paul Ltd for material from *Enemies of Promise* by Cyril Connolly, 'The Refutation of Idealism', 'The Conception of Reality' and 'The Conception of Intrinsic Value' from *Philosophical Studies* by G. E. Moore and *The Road to Serfdom* by F. A. Hayek; Martin Secker & Warburg Ltd and Brandt & Brandt for material from *Nineteen Eighty-Four* by George Orwell, copyright 1949 by Harcourt, Brace and World, Inc; *The Times* for an article *Law Report: Death of a Man and Wife at Sea*, published in *The Times*, 24 May 1962, and the literary executor, Mr Evelyn Waugh, for 'Idealism' by Mons. R. A. Knox from *In Three Tongues*.

PREFACE

Too often Philosophy tends to be regarded as a remote and abstruse subject which can only be profitably studied by the brilliant few. It seems to me that this is unfortunate and that philosophical matters are often less difficult and more important than is generally supposed.

We all philosophize whenever we attempt to handle abstract ideas and it may matter very much whether we do it well or badly. The object of this book is to introduce the reader gently to the activity of philosophizing and I hope that it may serve as some guide to what Philosophy is about both for those who are going to study the subject and for those who are not. I hope particularly that it may be of help to sixth form and other students who find themselves faced with what are generally regarded as border-line philosophical topics in their writing of general essays.

The first four chapters discuss the basic principles of the handling of words and ideas. In the fifth chapter I attempt to show these principles in use in the discussion of value judgements, a particularly important example of philosophizing which is very much within the experience of everybody. The selection of further topics to be discussed was inevitably somewhat abitrary. I chose 'Appearance and Reality' and 'Free Will and Determinism' because they seemed to me matters about which most people speculate at some time or other, and it might be useful and interesting to pursue those speculations further. These two chapters will probably be found rather harder than the rest of the book.

The Exercises at the end of chapters are designed to enable and encourage readers to practise the activity. They are of very varying difficulty and though I believe that most readers will find them helpful their omission need in no case hinder the understanding of subsequent chapters. Comments on most of the exercises are to be found at the end of the book. I have refrained from comment when the exercises are very easy or obvious, or when it is very much a matter of opinion. My comments are certainly not intended to be the last word on the matter, but I hope they may sometimes serve as the first words to start the discussion.

The Supplementary Passages at the end of some chapters are quotations from various sources to illustrate and illuminate points that have been raised, perhaps to explain them from a slightly different point of view.

Various friends have very kindly read and commented on some or all of the chapters at different stages. I owe a particular debt to Mr L. J. Russon and Professor Dorothy Emmet, but this is not to imply that they would necessarily wish to be associated with anything that I have written. The chapters, as they were being hammered into shape, were read and discussed with several groups of those whom I was trying to introduce to the subject at Winchester, and I am most grateful for the stimulating effect of their arguments and comments. I mention especially in this connexion Mr Francis Humphrys and Mr Christopher Sunter. And finally my grateful thanks to Mrs J. H. Preston for her skill and efficiency in deciphering and typing.

I

INTRODUCTION

MOST human beings are curious. Not, I mean, in the sense that they are odd, but in the sense that they want to find out about the world around them and about their own part in this world. They therefore ask questions, they wonder, they speculate. What they want to find out may be quite simple things: What lies beyond that range of hills? How many legs has a fly? Or they may be rather more complicated inquiries. How does grass grow? What is coal made of? Why do some liquids extinguish flames while others stimulate them? Or they may be more puzzling inquiries still: What is the purpose of life? What is it to be beautiful? What is the ultimate nature of truth? In what sense, if any, are our wills free?

To the first two questions the answers may be obtained by going and seeing, and catching one and counting, respectively. The answers to the next set of questions will not be so easy to find, but the method will be essentially the same. It is the method of the scientist, investigating, measuring, experimenting. A method that may reasonably be summed up by the phrase: 'Going and Seeing'. The last set of questions would normally be thought of as philosophical, and it would not be easy to find answers to them that would command general agreement. Some people would say that they are unanswerable. But those who have tried to answer them in the past have on the whole used the method of speculation rather than of investigation, of 'sitting and thinking' rather than of 'going and seeing'. 'Leisure', as

Thomas Hobbes remarked, 'is the mother of Philosophy'; the same relationship, it will be noted, as that which proverbially exists between necessity and invention. This should not be taken to imply that philosophers are not busy people, but their activity is likely to be mental rather than physical and this activity is likely to arise, not from a practical need to answer certain questions – as with necessity and invention – but from a natural curiosity which requires for its indulgence a measure of freedom from practical preoccupations.

It would be a misleading over-simplification, however, to identify science with investigation or going and seeing, and philosophy with speculation or sitting and thinking. The scientist who is investigating the world around him will certainly do some sitting and thinking about the results of his inquiries; and mathematicians, often as a result of pursuing lines of thought which seemed at first to have no practical applications, have made enormous contributions to modern discoveries in physics. The philosopher who is speculating about the nature of truth, though he may not do much going, is likely to do a certain amount of seeing. He must have some data for his reflections, even if it is only that which is provided by the fact that he is reflecting. And modern philosophers especially, as we shall see, often undertake detailed investigations into the ways in which language is used.

Nevertheless, it is on the whole true that for science the emphasis has been on investigation, and for philosophy on speculation, and philosophers have often been criticized for this reason.

It will be useful now to examine more closely what the word 'philosophy' has been and is used to describe.

It is a commonplace that the size of the estate covered by

this word today is very much smaller than it was. It might be argued, to make a further point by use of the same metaphor, that the fields that are left – as indeed the fields that are lost – are now very much more intensively cultivated than they used to be. It might also be argued that the picture of an estate is a misleading and question-begging one, whose use shows a misunderstanding of what it is that present-day philosophers are trying to do. But before we examine this question let us have a look at the estate of philosophy as it once was.

The word 'philosophy' was first used by the Greeks to mean the love of knowledge or wisdom. It is open to doubt whether man's wisdom has increased in the last two thousand years, but there can be no doubt at all about his increase in knowledge. An intelligent, well-educated person of two thousand years ago could reasonably be expected, if not to know all the knowledge there was, at least to be able to talk sense about any and every subject about which anything was known, into which investigations were being made, on which the thinkers of those days were exercising their minds or their imaginations. Aristotle, for example, who is generally regarded as one of the greatest philosophers of all time and as the founder of Logic, also wrote on Ethics, on Politics and on Poetics. He was also a leading scientist and two books of his in particular, *Physics* and *On the Heavens*, are said to have dominated science until the time of Galileo.

The point is that the estate of philosophy included almost all the fields of knowledge there were; in particular natural philosophy included science – what was known of the world about us, the knowledge which in modern times we have sub-divided further into chemistry, physics, zoology, botany and others. Nobody now would classify any of these sciences under the heading of philosophy. Their breaking away from the main estate has been gradual and piecemeal, and not a series of specific events to which definite dates could be attached. On the whole, each subject has achieved its independence as what was known about it grew, and as the method of inquirers in that field became organized and systematic. To some extent it would be true to say that each subject broke away as its problems were seen to be matters for going and seeing rather than sitting and thinking; for investigation rather than speculation.

What was left under the heading 'philosophy', then, consisted of those subjects in which the problems were still unsolved, or at least not definitely solved, and this is in part the explanation of the complaint that is made against philosophers that they never solve any problems. As soon as a problem or a set of problems is solved, or sometimes even seen to be soluble, the subject of which it forms a part ceases to be included under the comprehensive description of 'philosophy'.

A comparatively recent example of this process of achieving independence is provided by psychology. Another subject which is still in process of breaking away is political philosophy. And the name with which it has been christened in its new life is 'social science'. In both these cases we can see clearly how the fact that they are no longer in the estate of philosophy is due to the growing realization that the appropriate method of tackling their problems is that of going and seeing rather than sitting and thinking. For the social scientist the emphasis is on the observer with his notebook in the market-place, whereas the political philosopher has often not stirred much from his study.

What then is left to philosophy's estate?

There would be some difference of opinion as to whether

one still should include the cluster of inquiries which is usually called metaphysics. This has been described as an inquiry into the first whence and the last whither; an inquiry which is 'beyond' physics, which seeks to ask and answer the most ultimate and fundamental questions about the world in which we find ourselves, about space and time. It is obvious that since a portion of philosophy's estate was first described as metaphysics, physics has made tremendous advances. One has to go a good deal further and deeper therefore to get beyond physics. The physicist's description today of the world we see around us is so far from the common-sense assumptions that it seems at least doubtful whether he has left anything for the metaphysicist (or metaphysician, as he is somewhat irrationally called) to inquire into. It may also be doubted whether philosophical speculation is likely to yield any useful results in this field.

Another group of problems which are left for the philosopher to consider are those connected with our thinking. There is first the study of valid thinking or argument, which is called logic. And there is also the study of what has been called 'the latent structure of our actual thinking'. This is sometimes called epistemology, or theory of knowledge. It is a study, not so much of what we know or how we know, but rather of what it is to know.

There is also left for the philosopher the study of good and evil. This is called Ethics. As with everything that he studies, however, the philosopher is interested in the roots rather than the fruit; he is not concerned with an enumeration of good and bad actions or characteristics, nor on the whole is he concerned to make moral judgements or sermonize. In his capacity as a moral philosopher he is interested merely in the fundamental analysis, in what it is to be good or evil, right or wrong. He is investigating the concept of morality. It has always been assumed that this is a matter for sitting and thinking rather than for going and seeing, though clearly the thinker must have some knowledge and experience of the behaviour of human beings in contexts where the epithets 'good' and 'evil' are likely to be applied.

It has also traditionally been the task of the philsopher to examine and test the assumptions, explicit or implicit, which form the basis of other subjects. Books have been written about the philosophy of science, and the philosophy of mathematics; and these books attempt to investigate the fundamental, ultimate nature of these subjects. The concept of number or the concept of measurement is studied. What really is a number? What is one really doing when one measures? Much has also been written about the philosophy of history, attempting to investigate history at a deeper level, to ask just what a historical event or judgement is and to search for fundamental principles and tendencies.

Always the philosopher is expected to dig more deeply, analyse more clearly, to search for the real rather than the apparent; but he is expected to do it in realms where speculation rather than investigation is the appropriate method. And more and more, to quote G. J. Warnock, a modern philosopher, it is 'now generally agreed that the proper concern of philosophy is with concepts, with the ways in which and the means by which we think and communicate'. This more or less exclusive concern of many modern philosophers with the handling of concepts is indicative to some extent of a change in method. The tendency now is to look very much more carefully at the questions that are asked, and to claim that many of those which have puzzled mankind for centuries are foolish or improper or unanswerable. As Bertrand Russell has said:

'In philosophy, what is important is not so much the answers that are given, but rather the questions that are asked.' (*Wisdom of the West*, p. 19.)

This change in method is largely responsible for what seems to be a decline in the esteem in which philosophers and their speculations are generally held. The latter are certainly not regarded as very useful, though they are usually regarded among reasonably educated people as requiring a high degree of intelligence, of perhaps a rather specialized kind. The general view would almost certainly be that one has to be very clever to understand philosophy, though it might also be that one has to be rather foolish to want to understand it.

At least in the past, it is sometimes said, philosophers asked what are obviously very important and fundamental questions, even though they could not answer them. There were weighty, in every sense, treatises on what might be regarded as the Great Insolubles. And it was thought an important part of a gentleman's education that he should at any rate go through the motions of perusing at least a selected few of these tomes. That the problems were insoluble, even by the greatest minds of the age, engendered a proper feeling of what might be called general human humility. But at the same time there needed to be less of a particular feeling of humility at an individual failure to understand, when one realized that very few others understood them either. And since understanding led to no solution, such failure could hardly be considered of great importance.

But in the present, it is said, philosophy is reduced to linguistic analysis, a barren pursuit, a series of verbal quibbles, a picking of holes in the thoughts of others, notably the great ones of the past, with no positive contributions to offer whatever. That is the sort of thing which its detractors say about it. A description by one of its supporters goes thus: 'Philosophy', says Wittgenstein, 'is a battle against the bewitchment of our intelligence by means of language.' (*Philosophical Investigations*, Part I, paragraph 109.) And the same idea is also expressed by A. N. White-head, another famous philosopher of this century: 'The very purpose of philosophy is to delve below the apparent clarity of common speech.' (*Adventures of Ideas*, p. 214.)

If one thinks of philosophy in these terms it will perhaps now be apparent why we stated earlier that talk of the estate of philosophy would be regarded by many as an inapplicable and misleading metaphor. Instead of thinking of philos-ophy as a subject or collection of subjects, as a set of prob-lems to be solved, it would be more appropriate on the modern view to think of it as an activity; as a 'battle against bewitchment'; as a handling of concepts. In fact it would be more proper to think of the activity of *philosophizing*, rather than of the subject, philosophy.

The object of this book, then, is to assist people to philosophize in this sense, to show how concepts should be handled, and to show also how concepts have perhaps sometimes been wrongly handled in the past, owing very often to just that bewitchment of language to which Wittgenstein refers. This activity, we maintain, is both more important and less difficult than is often supposed. It is important because we all do it, and it makes a difference whether we do it well or badly. We are philosophizing whenever we speculate about justice, freedom, or honesty, and whenever we make a judgement that liberty must be defended or that tyranny cannot be tolerated. But this speculation is often carried out in a very inexpert manner. It is far more likely to be done effectively and sensibly if some attention has been given to certain basic principles; as with any other activity, physical or mental, most people will perform it more efficiently if they have first practised it under guidance. It may matter very much indeed, as a brief glance at history will show us, whether the results of these speculations are clear and sensible or muddled and foolish. To say that to philosophize is less difficult than is often supposed is of course to over-simplify. As with most activities there are grades of difficulty. But it has often seemed to be the case that the student of philosophy has been plunged at his first introduction to the subject into the deep end, and many people never discover that there is a shallow end too. It will be our aim to introduce the reader to fundamental and quite simple principles of philosophizing and then to move gradually to deeper water. What the beginner is likely to need above all is exercise and practice in order to make his thinking more flexible, more subtle, and therefore more effective; for this purpose many examples of varying difficulty are to be found throughout the book. No one need be put off if he finds that some of them are too difficult at the first attempt.

There is nothing new about the idea that the activity of philosophizing is more important than the subject, philosophy. Some two hundred years ago the great German philosopher, Immanuel Kant, told his pupils:

You will not learn from me philosophy, but how to philosophize, not thoughts to repeat, but how to think. Think for yourselves, enquire for yourselves, stand on your own feet. (Quoted in *Great Philosophers of the West* by E. W. F. Tomlin, p. 197.)

Nor must we think that there is anything very special about the method that is to be used for this activity. As Professor Karl Popper recently pointed out:

There is no method peculiar to philosophy. . . . And yet, I am quite ready to admit that there is a method which might be described as 'the one method of philosophy'. But it is not characteristic of philosophy alone; it is, rather, the one method of all *rational discussion*, and therefore of the natural sciences as well as of philosophy. The method I have in mind is that of stating one's problem clearly and of examining its various proposed solutions critically. K. R. POPPER, *The Logic of Scientific Discovery*, pp. 15–16.

It may be thought that this is not very original or startling; and the obviousness, even triteness, of these remarks may perhaps serve as some encouragement to anyone who had hitherto thought of philosophy as a specialized activity taking place in a rarefied atmosphere.

It is important to realize that the activity of philosophizing is not going to produce a set of cut-and-dried answers to clearly stated problems. We shall be moving in a world where 'one can't tell', 'I don't know', 'it all depends', 'it's a matter of opinion' will be essential and frequently recurring phrases. We shall hope to sort out and tidy up some problems and discover the kind of question that it makes sense to ask and the kind of answer that we can expect to get; we shall hope to discover something about the nature and the degree of the certainty that is attainable. And we shall hope to end up with more knowledge, more wisdom and a clearer understanding.

But if the ardent seeker after truth is not content with that, if he is only interested in answers that are right or wrong, if he wants final, conclusive certainty he must go elsewhere – to the study, for example, of pure mathematics. As he does so he will be shutting with a clang the door that leads to the world of 'it all depends'. And this will be a pity for it is the world in which we live.

LANGUAGE AND BEWITCHMENT

IT is not, I think, the case that all philosophizing is a battle against linguistic bewitchment, but it is nevertheless inescapable that language must be the medium of all philosophizing, or at least of all philosophizing that is communicated. We can only analyse concepts in terms of words, we can only learn to handle them by studying the use of language. As a preliminary to philosophizing in general, therefore, we shall investigate in this chapter the sense in which, and the ways in which, it may be said that our intelligences are bewitched by the use of language.

The study of the use of language is notoriously a delicate business. On the whole most people take it for granted and do not to any considerable extent subject the language they use and the ways in which they use it to a critical analysis or inquiry. This may be largely due to the fact that by the time an individual reaches the age of reflection or speculation he has learnt, by a process of which he has hardly been conscious at all, how to speak and use at least one language. We can most of us remember, if only perhaps rather vaguely, our first steps in Latin or Geometry, but I doubt whether anyone can remember his first steps in learning how to use his own language.

We take it for granted and are therefore inclined to regard it as something which is in a sense given, just 'there', as the facts of nature are given and 'there'. And because we have had no hand ourselves in the formation and construction of this language we tend to lose sight of what is perhaps the most important thing to remember about it, that we, mankind as a whole, invented and constructed the language and that we have the power collectively to change it as we will. We must never forget that we are or should be the masters, using language as a tool for thinking and communication, and we must try very hard to understand, and if necessary to resist, the subtle influences that words and language in general are capable of exerting on the thoughts and emotions of mankind.

We use language for certain purposes. We have just said that it is a tool for thinking and communication. The purposes for which we want to think or communicate are very various, but before we come to consider them it will be useful to say more about the distinction between them.

I am using the word 'thinking' in this context to include what is ordinarily called reflection. The distinction therefore between thinking and communication may be described as that between the private and public use of language. If I am reflecting to myself, using perhaps a combination of words and pictures, I am obviously entitled to use words exactly as I like and there is nothing to prevent me from using new words, or inventing a little private language of my own, perhaps in order to think about ideas or concepts for which the already existing language seems inadequate. If it amuses me to do so I can in my conversation with myself use words in a way which is quite different from that in which they are ordinarily used. A psychoanalyst might draw some interesting conclusions from my desire to do so, but it is perfectly possible for my reasoning to be no less effective and my reflection to be no less enjoyable because of this habit of mine. They might even be more so. I might be, as it were, exercising my mastery over language; stretching my intellect and my imagination.

But once this odd use of language on my part becomes public, once I start to use it for communication, then the case of course becomes quite different. If I am telling you what time the next train goes and I use the word 'three' to to denote the number 2 and the word 'four' to denote the number 3 and so on, the next train is likely to leave without you. I will not succeed in communicating with you unless I have first made it quite clear exactly how I intend to use the words. When A is communicating or attempting to communicate with B, A is using words or sentences to mean something, B is understanding something by the words or sentences he hears or reads. The communication is only fully effective if what B understands is the same as what A means. In simple cases ('The time is about quarter past eleven', 'The man over there in the green suit weighs over eighteen stone', 'We're having roast chicken and champagne for dinner tonight') it is not difficult to discover whether this is so; a misunderstanding or failure of communication is likely to be discovered quite easily. If B understands by 'past' what most people mean by 'to', the fact that he turns up half an hour late for his appointment at noon may lead to a sorting out of the entanglement. B may expostulate that so short and slim a man cannot possibly weigh anything like eighteen stone, and it may then emerge that A is colour-blind and uses 'green' to denote what is ordinarily understood by 'blue'. The disappointment of B at dinner time tonight when he is served with rabbit and Coca-Cola may lead to the realization, if they are frank with each other, that A uses the words 'chicken' and 'champagne' to mean any white meat and fizzy drink respectively.

But in more complicated cases ('The good is the enemy of the best'. 'In other words abstraction from the notion of "entry into the concrete" is a self-contradictory notion since it asks us to conceive a thing that is not a thing'), it may be no short and simple task to discover whether communication has been effective, and in the course of the investigation there may sometimes emerge some doubt as to whether A is absolutely clear about the ideas which he is using the words to represent.

The vital point is that men use words to mean various things. If communication on the whole is to be effective there must be built up an agreement that different people will use the same words for the same things. When the words are used to stand for concrete things or simple ideas, it is comparatively easy to ensure the building up and the understanding of this agreement without ambiguity, but when the words are used to stand for abstract or complex ideas such an agreement may be very hard to build up and, what is perhaps almost worse, it may be very difficult to judge whether such an agreement does or does not effectively exist.

ESSENTIAL MEANING

What we must get away from is the idea which in some form or other is very commonly held, often unconsciously, that words have an essential, real meaning if only we can discover what it is. This mistake is well exemplified by a quotation from Herbert Spencer: 'By comparing its meanings in different connexions and observing what they have in common we learn the *essential meaning* of a word.'

It is of course a sensible and useful thing to do to compare what a word is used to mean in different connexions and to observe what these meanings have in common. What we can learn from this procedure however is not 'the essential meaning', but simply what job we can employ this word to perform, what other people are likely to understand by it if we use it, what it will be sensible for us to understand by it when other people use it. We may find when we study the uses of a word in various contexts that they are so various, that it is used to mean so many different things by different people in different connexions, that as a tool for thinking or communication it is not always very effective. Consider the word 'good' for example. It is used as an adjective and as a noun, more frequently the former. It sometimes has moral implications when applied to people or their actions, but quite often not. 'Smith is a good man' in certain contexts and circumstances would be a sentence of moral praise, but in other contexts it might merely mean that he was a nice chap. In 'Jones is a good runner' the word would be very unlikely to carry any moral connotation, but would almost certainly indicate that Jones is capable of running fast. In most cases the word is used to indicate vague approval, admiration, commendation. It is also used even more vaguely in such phrases as 'a good many guns', 'a good deal of butter'.

One would be hard put to it to extract from its meanings in all these different connexions the 'essential meaning' to which Herbert Spencer refers. But it might be objected that many of these meanings are wrong meanings, that many of the uses are misuses. It is clearly not inconsistent with a belief in the 'essential meaning' of a word to suppose that it is sometimes incorrectly used through ignorance, stupidity or just perversity. The real, the essential meaning, it might be argued, is *there* all right, but it has been overlaid or obscured by the fools and knaves who have been misusing the word. The true, correct meaning may be discovered by looking it up in a 'good' dictionary or, what amounts to the same thing, by consulting the expert. The entry for the word 'good' even in so short a dictionary as the *Concise Oxford* covers well over a column. What it does is to record the various ways in which the word is used; there is no 'essential' meaning which emerges, though it might reasonably be argued that some of the usages are more 'correct' than others, that is, are more generally agreed upon by those who speak the language as a whole or just by those who have had more advanced, more expensive or 'better' educations.

The dictionary does more than record. It also guides, perhaps nearly dictates. It informs anyone who uses it of the meanings which are generally attached to words, and therefore informs readers, especially students, how they should use the word in future if they want to make themselves clearly understood. Changes, usually gradual ones, are taking place the whole time however in the ways in which words are used. These changes are seldom deliberate, they may be due to a failure of education, to ignorance or stupidity, but once they have taken place, once it has become the general practice to use a word with a new, slightly changed meaning, all the compiler of the dictionary can do is to record these changes.

It is interesting that in France there is an Academy which lays down the official meanings of words and publishes them. Again, in a sense, all that they do is to record the changes that take place, but it may well be that changes in usage are made less likely by the official laying down of the 'correct' meaning, by the fact, in other words, that the tacit agreement to which the users of the language have come as to the ways in which certain words are to be employed is set down in black and white.

In Great Britain, just as to a large extent our Constitution is unwritten and unofficial, so there is nothing officially laid down as to how our language should be used. Writers of dictionaries operate privately on their own initiative and although the best of them command considerable respect they have no official standing.

The realization that the concept of a word's essential meaning is a fallacious one, may tend to lead sometimes to a bouncing off to the opposite extreme. We like something fixed and correct to hang on to in our thinking, and if this is taken from us we may feel that everything is relative and in a state of flux, that we can use words as we like, that if words are invented by mankind we have as much right to invent them as anyone else, and if their meanings are continually being changed by alterations in usage why shouldn't we initiate these alterations as well as the next man. This is perhaps a natural reaction. The answer to someone who felt like this would be to point out that he can try if he likes, but he would run the risk of being misunderstood and failing to communicate effectively. Some people may feel distressed at the thought that it may be misleading to think of the one correct meaning which a word has, and that the criterion for deciding whether any one use is more correct than any other is simply that of general usage. But it may be some comfort to them to reflect that in considering this criterion it will obviously be true that the usages of those whose writings or whose utterances reach the largest audience will carry most weight in establishing a 'general' usage. The way in which Bernard Shaw used the English language when he wrote an essay which was read by half a million people is more likely to affect the general agreement about how words shall be used than the way in which John Smith uses it when he writes a letter to his grandmother. And in modern conditions it is worth noting also that the usages of those who address television audiences are likely to have a significant effect, perhaps more significant today than the written word.

It may be useful to consider an investigation of words that in general are used to convey approximately the same meanings: for example, 'deliberately' and 'intentionally'. It might be suggested that there are subtly different nuances. How is one to discover whether this is so or not? One possible way would be to consult the expert, ask the Professor of English. He might say that the word 'deliberately' carried a slightly aggressive connotation, that it was used of actions done on purpose, to annoy, and that 'intentionally' was more neutral, flat. Is his answer sufficient and satisfying? Is the expert right? We should surely try to investigate further, to see whether the words do in fact carry the slightly different shades of meaning which he says they do, and the test for this is whether people do in fact use them like this and whether they understand these differences when they read or hear them. Perhaps ideally we would have a squad of investigators who would watch and listen for the words to be used in writing and in talking and would try to elicit from writers, readers, speakers and hearers what they intended or understood. This method would be expensive and the population would have to be patient indeed for the investigators not to find it somewhat hazardous. In practice instead of waiting and watching for actual usages we should have to ask people, preferably a cross-section, how they are in the habit of using these words. This inquiry would not be as easy or as decisive as one might at first suppose. When we use different words to express subtly different shades of meaning we do it to some extent unconsciously and un-reflectively and quite a lot of self-examination, introspection, may be necessary before it can be clearly sorted out. Also, when we are using the spoken word, much of the meaning may be conveyed, by tone of voice, emphasis, expression, and it may be very difficult indeed to disentangle the extent to which we intend the shade of meaning to be conveyed by the word from the extent to which we intend it to be conveyed by other means. It is interesting that when we are talking we need words to convey slightly different meanings much less than when we are writing. Our voices, our intonations, our gestures can do some of the work that has to be done in writing by the words, the structure of the sentence and the punctuation.

Nevertheless let us suppose that we ask a random sample of people what difference, if any, there is between the meanings which they attach to or understand by the words 'deliberately' and 'intentionally'. (If we merely ask them the difference in meaning there would be a danger that they might think of the ways in which they 'ought' to use these words rather than of the ways in which they actually do use them; and this danger may not be entirely avoided by the rephrasing of the question.) It is likely that we will get a variety of answers. Some may say that they use the words indiscriminately, as synonyms; some may produce roughly the same answer as our Professor of English; others may produce a different answer. But suppose only a small percentage agree with the Professor, are the others wrong? Does this show that they have not been properly educated?

It will be noticed that the question has been phrased in such a way that, provided they have answered truthfully, there is no sense in which one can say that they are wrong. We are carefully not asking them how most people use the words or what is the correct meaning. What we are trying to find out is the difference in meaning which these words *in fact* convey, and the best way to do this is by direct investigation of particular cases of meaning being conveyed.

It might certainly be said however that disagreement with the Professor shows a lack of education and in a sense this may be quite true. A valid distinction can often be drawn between the majority usage of a word and its expert or educated usage. We must never lose sight however of the obvious fact that language is for communication and that to depart from majority usage is liable to lead to a failure of communication. If the majority of people think that William the Conqueror landed in England in A.D. 966 they are just wrong and their thinking does not make them right. But if the majority think that a word is used to convey a certain meaning, and, thinking this, use it thus, they are *right* and it is their thinking, and resultant action, which makes them right. It might still be true, however, that a minority of people, experts or better educated, use the word in a different way and effectively convey this different meaning among themselves. What generally happens is that the majority come to use words with wider, less specialized meanings, the subtle distinctions become blurred, the tools become blunter, less precise. If we can learn to use words in the same more specialized way our capacity for communication, but only to other members of the expert minority, will be enlarged. And if we learn to understand these subtle distinctions our capacity to understand and appreciate what some others have written, perhaps especially what the greatest writers in the language have written, will also be enlarged. It will be very much to our advantage that this should happen and it should be one of the most important things that we learn from our education. It will also be to the advantage of the community as a whole that subtle distinctions should be preserved, thus making possible the interchange of more precise and subtle ideas. The analogy here with a workman and his tools is, up to a point, a helpful one: the more accurate and finely graded set of tools he has the better his workmanship will be. But we note also an essential difference: however precise and subtly graded my verbal tools may be they are of no use at all for communication unless others have them too. And it is very difficult indeed to be sure that others have exactly or very nearly the same set, that the same shades of meaning are conveyed to the reader as were present in the writer's mind.

This is a difficulty that occurs in any writing that is at all complex, and it occurs perhaps most obviously in imaginative writing that is intended to evoke emotion or describe psychological states. There is a tendency for the ordinary reader or the literary critic to take out more than has been put in, to claim to find undercurrents of meaning which were not in the author's mind when he wrote it. Some experts would say that this is perfectly legitimate. Indeed it has been claimed that the 'best' poetry will use words and phrases which are deliberately *vaguely* evocative, leaving the reader, in fact *requiring* the reader, to use his imagination. In this respect it would be said to be like art. In an essay on 'The Artist in the Community' Charles Morgan makes his artist say 'I know what art is for. It is to enable men to imagine for themselves.' (*Liberties of the Mind*, p. 90.)

In an article in *Philosophy* (April 1954) Bernard Mayo suggests that no verse which has the qualities *clear, precise, unambiguous*, in any considerable degree is poetry. In such cases it would seem desirable that we should at any rate realize what is happening and that imaginative contributions by the reader should not be claimed as discoveries about the author's intentions.

A similar process happens on a larger scale, but on the whole as an elaborate joke, when the Sherlock Holmes society is formed and its members speculate about the characteristics, history and antecedents of the fictitious character Sherlock Holmes. It sometimes happens rather more seriously when the plays, for example, of Shakespeare, are subjected to an over-elaborate investigation, and conclusions are drawn about the characters which are very unlikely indeed to have been in the mind of their creator.

But whatever may be thought about the desirability of the reader's imagination supplementing what the poet, the novelist or the dramatist had in mind when he wrote, there can surely be no doubt that in any communication that claims to be rational, to explain, or to argue a case, it is desirable that what the reader understands should be as nearly as possible identical with what the writer meant.

When we are examining works that were written a long time ago it will be important to know how words were used then: and we shall only be able to discover this by studying examples of the use of the word in different contexts and perhaps by different people. We shall have to remember that it is probable that then as now there was not complete consistency about its use, and our inquiry will be made more difficult by the possibility that the usages of many of the other words which provide the contexts of the one we are investigating may have changed too.

It is usual to speak and write as though the usages of those who have what is normally regarded as the best education should take precedence over others, should be regarded as more correct and generally to be preferred. This is clearly perfectly reasonable. As we have already pointed out these usages are likely to be more subtle, more useful. Also those

who have been educated more are on the whole likely to
read and write more than those who have been educated
less, and what they say is likely to reach a larger audience.
It is clearly desirable, as we have seen, that usages should
not change too much or vary too much, and it is therefore
useful to regard the usage of the educated man as a kind of
norm. But it cannot be repeated too often that usage is the
only test. It is no good saying that a word means such-and-
such if people on the whole do not in fact use it this way or
understand it this way. It often happens that usages are
different and this is certainly regrettable; where this is so
the important thing is to be aware of it and it may sometimes
be possible to take steps to persuade people to use the word
more consistently.

There is a tendency, perhaps especially a modern one, to
examine words minutely, as it were through a microscope,
to see what different shades of meaning they carry. But the
results of such an analysis are only valid if they do in fact
represent the ways in which people, even if only a minority
of people, use the words. Still less will it be legitimate to go
on to infer from these alleged minute differences of meaning
facts about the nature of the reality which these words
purport to describe. The analogy does not work. We can
discover facts about flies by examining them through a
microscope, because there are microscopic facts about
flies to be discovered. But it seems very doubtful whether
there are often analogously microscopic facts about usages
to be discovered. Our usages on the whole are not sufficiently precise to merit so detailed an investigation.
Certainly they must be examined, with care and thought,
but again we cannot expect to take out more than has been
put in. An impressionist painting of the Parthenon will not,
however many times magnified, reveal the writing on the

wall. An X-ray photograph of the bust of Napoleon will not tell us whether he had a tumour on the brain.

We have dwelt on what might be called the fallacy of essential meaning at some length. Our excuse for doing so is that though almost everyone will agree that it is a fallacy when their attention is called to it, there is a danger still that only lip-service will be paid to the correct view. For many people the fallacious way of looking at things is so deeply ingrained that they find it very difficult to rid themselves of the conceptions and assumptions which it entails and will often go on talking and thinking as though there were a real meaning there if only they could find it.

THE DIFFERENT PURPOSES FOR WHICH LANGUAGE IS USED

We distinguished earlier between the private or reflective use of language and its public use for communication. It will be useful now to consider some of the different purposes for which communication is required, and while we do this we shall consider also in which of these purposes bewitchment is likely to result and where it is likely to be most dangerous.

Language is used first of all to give simple factual information. Closely allied with this is its use to give simple commands ('Shut the Door') or ask simple questions ('What time is dinner?'). No particular difficulties or complications are likely to arise about these uses. They may still form the subject of interesting philosophical analysis but in our ordinary everyday life we are not likely to be bemused or bewitched by our use of language for these purposes. The fact that it may be used to misinform as well as to inform need not interest us now.

Language may also be used to persuade. The arts of the

orator or the politician may be employed through the medium of language to persuade people to think or act in a way in which they otherwise would not. This persuasion will often be rational and directed towards good ends, but it may sometimes contain an element of deception; the language may be used to dull the intelligence and appeal to the emotions. Sometimes the speaker or writer may be doing this deliberately, sometimes he may, in a sense, be bewitching himself with the language he is using.

We have already referred to the use of language to express or convey or evoke emotion. In such cases it might certainly be said that the writer may be using it, perhaps deliberately, to bewitch our intelligences. But it is a bewitchment of a kind rather different from that to which Wittgenstein was referring.

There is finally the use of language to think and to convey one's thoughts – in the present context there is not much point in separating these two; its use in speculating and in following trains of thought about complicated and abstract matters; its use in analysing and explaining; its use in examining the different uses of language.

It is in this last, not very precisely defined, use that important bewitchments are most likely to occur.

'BEWITCHMENT'

Let us examine a little more closely what we mean by 'bewitchment' and in what ways it can and does take place.

The sort of bewitchment to which Wittgenstein was referring would be exemplified at a very elementary and unsophisticated level if we supposed that because the word 'griffin' exists there must exist also the animal for which the name stands.

In other words if, as a result of language and the way in which it is used, we are misled about the nature of reality, the way things in fact are, then our intelligences may be said to have been bewitched by language.

'The word exists, therefore the thing exists' is not likely to mislead us at the level of fabulous animals, but it can very easily do so at a more complicated, abstract level. It might be argued for example that the fallacy, which we have been discussing in the last few pages, of a word's essential meaning is partly due to the fact that we talk about 'the meaning of a word'. If we talk about the word's meaning, it must be *there*, so we set about finding it, and the search goes on. If, instead, we had talked about the way in which we use a word we should have been more likely to think about it the right way.

But obviously it can be further argued that people talked in the first instance about the 'meaning of a word' because they supposed that that way of talking about it represented the correct way of thinking about it. The error of thought preceded and was responsible for the misleading language. Whichever error came first there seems to be a strong case for saying that they are closely bound together.

Modern scientists have pointed out the dangers to our thinking which follow from supposing that because the word exists some mysterious entity or what Newton called 'occult quality' exists also. Words like 'current' as applied to electricity, and 'electricity' itself are examples. The existence of the word leads naturally to the question 'What *is* electricity?' and to ask this question assumes a misleading materialistic model. What scientists try to do instead is, as Professor J. Z. Young said, (Reith Lectures, 1950) 'to find a language that will more directly describe our observations'. And he goes on 'We find that we can talk about electricity quite easily without asking what it is made of, or whether its flow is like water. In fact, provided we can accurately describe the conditions and relations in which electrical phenomena occur, we can do much better without the old models.' (Further passages illustrating this point will be found on pages 69–70.)

These are examples of our being perhaps deceived about the way things are, of our thinking being incorrect, because of the existence of a word. It may also happen, as we shall suggest later, as a result of the structure of the language. In every case however it seems probable that the fact that these misleading words or ways of talking or writing exist, indicates that at one time they reflected the way people thought about reality. We may come to believe now that these thoughts are erroneous, but the fact that the errors are, as it were, *embedded* in the language, and are often basic to our thinking may make it very difficult indeed for us to detect them. As Bentham said 'Error is never so difficult to be destroyed as when it has its roots in Language.' The errors that are embedded in Language may be the results of mistaken thinking, they may also result from a lack of thought. When one considers the rather haphazard way in which languages are bound to grow, it is obvious that words and ways of speaking do not always represent a clear thinking out of the problems which may underlie the things and ideas which are being described. We can look around us and watch language growing most obviously perhaps in the form of slang; this certainly seems to be largely haphazard and we would hardly expect it to represent reality accurately. And the slang of one generation often becomes the accepted phraseology of the next.

At the opposite extreme we can see professors in general

and scientists in particular coining words and phrases which will, on the whole, be thought out and intended to assist those who use them to think accurately about whatever is being described.

We must be careful to steer a middle course between supposing that the assumptions of language are always wrong and that they are always right, for a middle course is certainly what one would expect to be correct. Men after all use words to *describe*, to some extent to *explain*, what they find in nature. It has certainly not been the case that men have always described or explained correctly what they have found, and it is not surprising therefore that language as a whole often carries erroneous implications. On the other hand they have certainly not always been wrong. A close study of the language will show us how men have thought, but it will not of itself provide much evidence as to what is right. Modern philosophers are sometimes accused of placing too much faith in the assumptions of language. Ernest Gellner in his *Words and Things* (p. 255) talks of 'the Wittgensteinian idea that ordinary language is always and perfectly in order', though in doing so he refers to the shift from this idea 'to the *apparently* weaker and less exposed idea that ordinary language is only very, very likely to be right in the distinctions it draws'. And G. J. Warnock in his *English Philosophy since 1900* expresses a similar idea. He writes:

Language does not develop in a random or inexplicable fashion. It is to be *used* for a vast number of highly important purposes; and it is at the very least unlikely that it should contain either much more or much less than these purposes require. . . . If so, the existence of a number of different ways of speaking is very likely indeed to be an indication that there is a number of different things to be said.

And again 'where the topic at issue really is one that does constantly concern most people in some practical way . . . then it is certain that everyday language is as it is for some extremely good reason'.

It might be remarked that though the reasons may be 'good' in the sense that they are valid, that they really are responsible for the language being as it is, and that they seemed good and correct to the individuals or the generation that was responsible for the language, they need not be good in the sense that they are in fact correct, or thought by us to be correct today.

The word 'witch' exists for what was at one time the extremely good reason that people thought that some females practised an evil form of magic. This belief is certainly less generally held today, so that though the reason for the word is in a sense 'extremely good' the study of the word or the language will not necessarily lead us to the true facts about reality, but only to facts about what mankind at one time thought reality was like.

MANY MASQUERADING AS ONE

Let us consider now other kinds of bewitchment, other ways in which mistakes may be embedded in the language. Confusion may sometimes arise because the same word is used to mean different things. The difficulty may perhaps be illuminated by the consideration of an obvious example. If, in a community, there are three people called John Smith who resemble each other closely and are in the habit of dressing alike, one might easily suppose, unless one happened to meet more than one of them at the same time, that there was only one John Smith. Such an error could clearly lead to confusion and muddle and could only be sorted out either by explanation, or by the appearance of all three of them together. In a sense the three John Smiths might masquerade as one. This confusion could not arise if they looked quite different, if one was black, one yellow and one white. In the same way many ideas may masquerade as one idea if they have the same name, but confusion is only likely to arise if they resemble each other closely. The word 'investment' for example is used popularly to describe the action of a private individual in buying stocks and shares, and it is also used by economists to describe the action of a company in expanding its factories or improving its machinery. These meanings are closely linked and in certain circumstances what they describe may be different facets of the same event, but it is often exceedingly confusing that the same word has the two different senses – for example a higher rate of interest may tend to encourage investment in one sense, for individuals will be offered a higher reward for saving and 'investing', and discourage it in the other, for industrialists will be asked to pay a higher price for borrowing and 'investing'. In general the use of the same word to mean slightly different things is a frequent cause of fallacious arguments and often one which it is by no means easy to detect. When the meanings differ widely the masquerade is unlikely to be effective. The fact that the word 'arms' is used to mean weapons of war as well as human limbs is unlikely to lead to confusion. Indeed it is much more likely to lead to a joke, as when we are told of Ben Battle: 'A cannon ball took off his legs, so he laid down his arms.' The existence of words with widely different meanings forms the basis of a considerable proportion of English humour. In fact just how considerable is rather a sobering thought.

ONE MASQUERADING AS MANY

It is also possible to have the bewitchment of the one masquerading as many. This may happen with people as a result of deliberate intent. Bill Jones the polygamist may under different names have three wives in different towns. An author may write under different noms-de-plume for different purposes, and the public may be led to suppose erroneously that there is not one writer but three writers. In most languages, perhaps especially in the English language, it is commonplace for there to be more than one word for the same, or very nearly the same, idea. Synonyms abound, but they need give rise to no particular difficulty or confusion as long as they are seen to be synonyms. At a trivial level confusion may temporarily arise because of the convention, especially among journalists, of avoiding repetition. If one reads in an account of a football match references in the same paragraph to 'the talented inside-left', 'the wily Aberdonian', 'the Scottish wizard', it may not be immediately obvious that the same individual, MacTavish, is being talked about on each occasion. This kind of confusion is less likely to arise with ideas, though it is often useful to ask ourselves in our thinking and our reading whether two words or phrases are different ways of describing the same thing or ways of describing different things.

CLEAR-CUT DIVISIONS AND INSENSIBLE GRADATIONS

We use words to label and to classify what we find in the world around us. It is for a great many purposes convenient to place things in separate compartments or pigeon-holes. Very often we find in nature divisions which are completely clear-cut, for example the division between two-legged animals and four-legged animals. There would also be a clear-cut division between both these and three-legged animals, if any such were to be found.

Although some divisions in nature are clear-cut and can therefore be described easily in words, many, perhaps most, of them are not. We find in nature the whole time insensible gradations between the more and the less, between black and white, solid and liquid, fat and thin, heavy and light, old and young, hot and cold, clever and stupid, generous and greedy, sane and insane. When we attach labels such as 'bipeds', 'quadrupeds', 'cats', 'dogs', 'roses', 'trousers', the clear-cut divisions which the labelling implies are entirely appropriate for the facts as we find them in nature. There is a danger, however, that we may come to think that the act of labelling implies a clear-cut division where none exists.

It can be seen that the pairs quoted in the preceding paragraph vary in the extent to which the insensible gradations are capable of measurement. As we proceed from light to heavy there is a lower limit of being completely light, or having no weight, but there is no upper limit of being completely heavy. The position which any particular object has on the scale can be measured to varying degrees of accuracy and a numerical value in pounds, tons, grammes, or other units of weight can be attached to it. It is not likely that anyone will have any difficulty in realizing that the words 'light' and 'heavy' are relative, and that which one is applied to a given object will depend on the circumstances and context. A heavy man might weigh the same as a light car. This would be because the man was heavier than most men and the car lighter than most cars. It is probably on the whole not the case that people are bewitched by this practice, though perhaps there are sometimes foolish discussions or arguments as to which of the two labels should be attached to a particular person or object. It might be hard to see how language can could have done better about this. It is useful to have vague words as long as it is realized that they are vague; troubles are only likely to arise if vague words are treated as though they were precise. With the words heavy and light it is not usually desirable to draw a line between them though it is obviously perfectly easy to do so if thought to be necessary. Bewitchment however is not likely to arise from having clear-cut division words applying to an insensible gradation category if it is always possible by going and measuring or weighing to decide exactly where on the scale a given object belongs.

But suppose this is not possible. Consider the words 'sane' and 'insane'. It would I suppose be agreed by most experts, firstly that this is a case where insensible gradations apply rather than clear-cut divisions; and secondly that it is not possible to attach precise numerical values to people to indicate their degree of sanity; it is perhaps to some extent a matter of opinion. It is held to be desirable for certain purposes, mainly legal ones, to draw a line dividing the sane from the insane, and it is notoriously a very difficult matter indeed to agree on what criteria to apply, where and how to draw the line in such a way that it will be possible to decide on which side of it to put any given person.

There are of course several difficulties intertwined here. There is the question as to whether insensible gradation or clear-cut division is the right way of looking at it; there is the question of the extent to which it is a matter of fact or of opinion; and there is the question with which we are mostly concerned here of the extent to which the existence of words for just the two classifications has influenced our thinking about it and prevented us from considering sufficiently how important it may be to look at the matter from the insensible gradation point of view. People will clearly vary considerably as to the extent to which they will take the view, when the possibility is pointed out to them, that perhaps in many respects their thinking *has* been influenced in this way. They will not necessarily be right about it, they may not even be the best judges, but their evidence will be interesting and important.

There can be no doubt at all, however, that a great number of futile and necessarily inconclusive arguments and discussions do in fact take place in which the contestants are disputing as to which of two clear-cut division labels shall be attached to a person, a thing, or a concept, and in which the very obvious truth that it is all a matter of degree seems to be overlooked.

Another way of expressing this is to say that our language and our logic tend to be two-valued whereas nature tends to be multi-valued. One of the laws of thought enunciated by Aristotle was the law of the excluded middle: 'Everything is either A or not A.'

In a sense this is certainly and obviously true, or can be made so by a careful definition and agreement as to what it is to be A. 'Everything is either made of wood or not made of wood' (but we must agree about what we are to say of things that are partly made of wood). 'Everything is either in Hampshire or not in Hampshire' (but we must agree about whether the vultures hovering in the air above Winchester are *in* Hampshire). But even in these comparatively simple cases, and far more in such trickier cases as we have been considering ('Everybody is either sane or insane'), we see that this 'law' can be distinctly misleading. It can often only be made true by definitions which are artificial and unsatisfactory, which introduce clear-cut distinctions where none are in nature. Indeed to such an extent is this true that logicians talk about the *fallacy* of the excluded middle, of supposing that there are always only *two* values, A and not A, true and false, instead of many intervening values. Obviously the more firmly our logic and language are two-valued the more likely it is that our thinking will be rigid and dogmatic. It has been claimed (Stuart Chase, *The Power of Words*, p. 106) that Chinese is a multi-valued language and that as a result the Chinese have been better able to appreciate the intervening shades of grey between the extremes of black and white, and their thought has been more flexible and more tolerant.

We must be careful, however, not to overstate the degree of bewitchment that may arise from the shortcomings of our language in this respect. There certainly seem to be many cases where we clearly recognize that it is all a matter of degree, and in which this recognition is reflected in the language we use.

Consider for example the adjectives 'empty' and 'full'. Everyone would, I think, immediately agree that it is perfectly clear that as applied to most things there are many, usually infinitely many, gradations between the two extremes. We describe these either vaguely, as in 'fairly empty', 'almost full', or more precisely 'three-quarters full'. There does not seem to be any kind of bewitchment here. We have a clear concept which we understand completely and we have a vocabulary which we can use about it, vaguely if that is all that is wanted, or precisely if that is necessary. It is made easier by the fact that in this case the gradations are usually capable of numerical measurement.

Let us consider another pair where no numerical measurement is possible: 'comfortable' and 'uncomfortable'. Again most people would probably readily agree that there are innumerable gradations between the two. In this case neither word represents a definite clear-cut limit to the scale, as do full and empty. In recognition of the fact that it is a matter of degree the adjective is qualified by such words as 'fairly'. It will also easily be recognized that whether for example a chair is comfortable or not is a matter of opinion. Altogether the concept of comfort is one about which people do not find it hard to think clearly.

We certainly cannot claim, therefore, that our intelligences are always bewitched by the fact that the labels available are clear-cut division ones though the reality is represented by insensible gradations. Undoubtedly in some matters we manage to see things clearly in spite of this and our inability to see things clearly in other matters may therefore be due at least in part to other causes. But there is no reason why there should be a comprehensive answer to this question. Some people may be bewitched by this, others not, some may have thrown off the bewitchment, others have never needed to. To decide to what extent language bewitchment is responsible for some faulty thinking is not possible nor, perhaps, is it very important. What does matter is to realize that here is a bunch of concepts about which we may not always think very clearly and correctly and that we are more likely to do so if in examining the concept we also examine carefully the language which we use about it.

It may be worth noting here the point that it is often convenient for various purposes to classify under general headings. The early economists, for example, found it helpful to consider the factors of production under the four headings: land, labour, capital and enterprise. This represented a convenient way of looking at things, it spot-lighted differences of a kind that were relevant and helpful to the methods of inquiry into the subject-matter. For other purposes, for other methods of inquiry, a quite different classification might have been more useful. It is important to realize that such classifications, though they may certainly correspond to real differences, are matters of convenience and need not be regarded too rigidly. The divisions between the categories might not be sharply defined, and the categories might not between them exhaust all the possibilities. Similar classifications for convenience are familiar to anyone who has a lot of papers to file and a conscientious secretary may get very worried about the heading under which a given document is to be put. It would be important for her to realize that the *right* answer is the *convenient* answer, that convenience is related to purpose, that in the last resort this may be a matter of opinion, and that it will be very much in her interests to try to ensure that her opinion coincides with that of her employer.

THE STRUCTURE OF THE SENTENCE

Another way in which it has been suggested that language may bewitch our intelligences is by the structure of the sentence. A common form of sentence in many languages, but not all, is of the type 'Some roses are red'. There is here a subject, 'some roses'; a predicate 'red'; and a part of the verb 'to be'. It used to be claimed (by Aristotle and his followers) that all statements or propositions could usefully be put in this form, and for a very long time it was considered an important part of the study of Logic to do so. Several consequences may reasonably be claimed to have followed from this. In the first place all statements would appear to be attributing a quality to a thing (in the above example the quality of redness to roses). This tended to encourage the notion that there were to be found in nature 'substances' 'possessing', in some sense, a variety of properties, and made it seem to be correct to think of the quality 'redness' existing apart from the 'substance', and then being exemplified in these particular red roses. This is not now thought to be a useful way of thinking about the matter; it leads to the twin errors of supposing that there are universals – e.g. redness – in some way existing or subsisting apart from red objects, and of supposing that there is a fabulous 'substance' existing apart from the qualities which it possesses. These mistakes are almost certainly due to a very considerable extent to the errors of language. As Bertrand Russell has said: '"Substance" ... is a metaphysical mistake due to transference to the world-structure of the structure of sentences composed of a subject and predicate.' (*History of Western Philosophy*, p. 225.) This view is supported by the fact that, as Aldous Huxley says in his *Adonis and the Alphabet* (p. 189),

In Chinese there are no fixed parts of speech, sentences do not take the subject-predicate form and there is no verb meaning 'to be'. Consequently, except under foreign influence, Chinese philosophers have never formulated the idea of 'substance' and never projected the word into the universe.

But even though it may be true that the idea of 'substance' and the concept of universals are perhaps derived from and at least supported by the formation of language, it might still be argued that the language came to be like that because the generations constructing it thought that reality was like that. The Chinese had different views about reality and therefore the structure of their language is different. We shall perhaps never be able to know to what extent these differences in structure were accidental and to what extent they represented differences in views about the nature of reality; but what we can be reasonably sure about is that once the language was formed its structure inevitably affected, almost certainly without their being aware of it, the assumptions and the thinking of those who used it.

Another way in which the form of the Aristotelian proposition may have bewitched our intelligences is as follows. The sentence 'This table is four feet long' has the appearance of being the same sort of sentence as 'These strawberries are very nice.' In the one case the property of length, precisely specified (four feet), is attributed to this table; in the other case the property of niceness, vaguely specified (very), is attributed to these strawberries. It would be readily agreed, however, that what is said in the second sentence would be more properly stated by saying 'I like these strawberries'. The four feet of length would be generally thought of as a public, objective, fact; whereas the 'niceness (very)' would be thought of as a private, subjective, opinion. By putting the statement in the Aristotelian form, however, there is a danger that what is really subjective may be made to appear as objective, that matters of opinion may be made to appear as matters of fact, that what is really relative may be made to appear as absolute. It is not very likely that any bewitchment will result from talking about the niceness of strawberries. If it does it is likely to be temporary and easily removable; a small amount of reflection makes it obvious. But when we come to dealing with matters where it is not so obvious whether it is a matter of opinion, the structure of the sentence may to some extent prejudice the issue for some people; there may in fact be a bewitchment. Whether 'beauty' should properly be thought of as subjective or objective, for example, is a difficult question which we shall be discussing later, but the views of many people about this are almost certainly affected by the fact that they will most frequently have heard it talked about in objective terms, and this fact may at least in part be due to the whole Aristotelian sentence-structure inheritance.

Our language, then, shows us how we or our predecessors have labelled or categorized reality, the divisions we have made, the relationships we have inferred or assumed, the classifications which it has been convenient to make. By studying language we can learn much about the thought-patterns of our predecessors. Sometimes perhaps we will come to the conclusion that these thought-patterns are wise and appropriate, and sometimes we will come to the opposite conclusion, but these are matters which must be judged on their own merits. We must be very careful indeed not to claim to extract from the study of the language more than is really there.

As we move on to the practice of philosophizing, to the study and analysis of concepts, we shall be continually on the look out for the bewitchments of language. We will certainly find that, in spite of the claim by Wittgenstein that Philosophy is the battle against this bewitchment, many of these bewitchments, as indeed Wittgenstein would surely agree, have been created and perpetuated by philosophers. In other words it is certainly true that philosophizing has been, and perhaps to some extent is bound to go on being, both the bewitchment and the unbewitchment. As Bishop

Berkeley put it: 'We have first raised a dust and then complain we cannot see.' (Introduction to *Treatise Concerning the Principles of Human Knowledge*, paragraph 3.)

The critical climate of opinion in this country today is such that it seems unlikely that any present-day writers will rival the great metaphysical bewitchers of the past. There is nothing new about the view that an essential basis for philosophizing must be a study of language, but it seems to be a view held more strongly by a greater number of people today than ever before. Some critics would take the view that there is a danger that the study of language may be thought to be the whole of Philosophy, but this view may be based on a misunderstanding of what it is to examine a concept. The philosopher who studies language is inevitably at the same time studying what it is that the language is about. We discuss this point in the next chapter.

Exercises

1. Consider the differences, if any, between the ways in which you use the members of the following sets of words:
    i. surprised, astonished, amazed, astounded
    ii. prevent, hinder
    iii. respect, regard
    iv. risk, hazard
    v. show, demonstrate
    vi. teach, instruct
    vii. delight, joy, exultation, rapture

2. Analyse the different ways in which the italicized words are used in the following passages:

(*a*) i. Clutterworthy and I were both staying at the *same* hotel in August.

ii. Mrs Clutterworthy and my wife were both wearing the *same* hat at Ascot.

iii. All civilized nations have basically the *same* moral code.

iv. The Highway Code is the *same* as it was last year.

(b) i. The rose *is* red.

ii. Twice two *is* four.

(c) i. I rely on your good *faith*.

ii. I accepted unquestioningly the *faith* of my fathers.

iii. I have complete *faith* in Dr Proctor's pills.

(d) i. If you are a *real* smoker ... is the cigarette made specially for you.

ii. Is that a *real* rat or am I just seeing things?

iii. The *real* problem is ...

(e) i. 'In later years I think we realized the true *meaning* of sport is to win.' (DANNY BLANCHFLOWER as reported in the *Listener*, 17 October 1963.)

ii. He gave me a look that was full of *meaning*.

iii. A mechanistic universe is without *meaning*.

iv. He doesn't seem to understand the *meaning* of what happened last week.

v. I don't know the *meaning* of any Russian words.

3. The perfect use of language is that in which every word carries the meaning that it is intended to, no less and no more. In this verbal exchange Fleet Street is a kind of Bucket Shop which unloads words on the public for less than they are worth and in consequence the more honest literary bankers, who try to use their words to mean what they say, who are always 'good for' the expressions they employ, find their currency constantly depreciating. There was a time when this was not so, a moment in the history of language when words expressed what they meant and when it was impossible to write badly. This time I think was at the end of the seventeenth and the beginning

of the eighteenth century, when the metaphysical conceits of the one were going out and before the classic tyranny of the other was established. To write badly at that time would involve a perversion of language, to write naturally was a certain way of writing well. CYRIL CONNOLLY, *Enemies of Promise*, pp. 22–3.

Discuss the meaning and the possibility of there being a time 'when words expressed what they meant and when it was impossible to write badly'.

4. Discuss the argument of the following passage:

It is sometimes said that words mean what they are used to mean and that essential meaning is a myth. This idea is one more example of the deplorable modern tendency to try to substitute the relative for the absolute. The fallacy can perhaps most simply be exposed by the use of an analogy.

Words are often usefully compared with a carpenter's tools; they are the tools of thinking and communication. Now it may happen that in a certain community chisels come to be used to insert and extract screws, they are *used* as screw-drivers and it might be argued that in a literal sense they have become, they *are*, drivers of screws, screw-drivers. It would, I think, be readily agreed, however, that though they are being used by the clumsy and the foolish to drive screws they remain, in an important sense, chisels and nothing, short of destruction, can take from them their essential chiselhood. This would still be true even though there were only a few people, or even no one, capable of recognizing this. In the same way, although a word may be used by the uneducated and the stupid with a different, a debased, meaning, it retains and must always retain its own true, essential meaning even though there are very few, or none, who understand it. It is curious that those same people, who are ready to use the analogy of tools when it suits their purpose, are not prepared to follow the analogy to its logical conclusion, the convincing demonstration of the reality of essential meaning.

5. No scientist has ever directly observed an atom, a nucleus of an atom, or an electron. He observes what he interprets as changes in entities which he or one of his predecessors has invented. But by making use of those entities, he provides the data needed to build chemical factories, nuclear power stations and electronic computers. That, in a crude form, is the test of usefulness.

While reassured by the existence of practical devices that work, a scientist may yet feel a concept to be justified for a time if it merely helps him to think. (From an article on 'The Philosophy of Science', *The Times*, 11 May 1962.)

A philosopher may similarly say that a concept or the invention of an entity may help him to think. Discuss the extent to which, in philosophizing, the test of usefulness can be applied.

6. The ancient Greeks, as well as all Western peoples today, say 'the light flashed'. Something has to be there to make the flash; 'light' is the subject; 'flash' is the predicate. The whole trend of modern physics, however, with its emphasis on the *field*, is away from subject-predicate propositions. A Hopi Indian, accordingly, is the better physicist when he says '*Reh-pi*' – 'flash!' – one word for the whole performance, no subject, no predicate, and no time element. (Children tend to do this too.) In Western languages we are constantly reading into nature ghostly entities which flash and perform other miracles. Do we supply them because our verbs require substantives in front of them? STUART CHASE, *The Power of Words*, p. 103.

Discuss the extent to which we may be misled in our thinking by this. Can you think of other examples?

7. Discuss the extent to which the existence of mysterious entities or occult qualities is assumed in the following sentences. Might they be misleading because of this? Consider how you would rephrase them to avoid it.

   i. What's happened to his confidence?
   ii. She seems to have found a new serenity.
   iii. How much personality has he got?
   iv. He has spent his whole life in search of the ultimate reality.
   v. Did you notice his integrity?
   vi. Let us ask what Progress is in itself.

8. The Bewitchments we have been considering have on the whole been caused by what might be thought of as accidents of language. It will be interesting to take a look now at a fictitious example where language is deliberately designed to cause people to think along certain lines.

The following extract is from George Orwell's *Nineteen Eighty-four*:

The purpose of Newspeak was not only to provide a medium of expression for the world-view and mental habits proper to the devotees of Ingsoc [English Socialism] but to make all other modes of thought impossible. It was intended that when Newspeak had been adopted once and for all and Oldspeak forgotten, a heretical thought – that is, a thought diverging from the principles of Ingsoc – should be literally unthinkable, at least so far as thought is dependent on words. Its vocabulary was so constructed as to give exact and often very subtle expression to every meaning that a Party Member could properly wish to express, while excluding all other meanings and also the possibility of arriving at them by indirect methods. This was done partly by the invention of new words, but chiefly by eliminating undesirable words and by stripping such words as remained of unorthodox meanings, and so far as possible of all secondary meanings whatever. To give a single example. The word *free* still existed in Newspeak, but it could only be used in such statements as 'This dog is free from lice', or 'This field is free from weeds'. It could not be used in its old sense of 'politically free' or 'intellectually free' since political and intellectual freedom no longer existed even as concepts, and were therefore of necessity nameless. . . . Newspeak was designed not to extend but to *diminish* the range of thought, and this purpose was indirectly assisted by cutting the choice of words down to a minimum. Op. cit. pp. 241–2.

We have suggested that the existence of a word may make people think, possibly mistakenly, that a corresponding entity exists. Discuss the extent to which Newspeak would be likely to succeed in restricting the range of thought, abolishing ideas, by attempting to abolish words and restrict their usages.

9. Consider to what extent a common property is being ascribed when one talks about:

i. a red frock, a red cricket-ball, a red herring;
ii. a real table, a real artist, a real advantage;
iii. absolute misery, absolute power, absolute beauty.

10. Discuss the problems raised by the following extracts from Wittgenstein's *Philosophical Investigations*:

i. Compare –
(*a*) 'This sentence makes sense.' 'What sense?'
(*b*) 'This set of words is a sentence.' 'What sentence?'
Part I, paragraph 502.
ii. Could someone understand the word 'pain' who had *never* felt pain? Is experience to teach me whether this is

so or not? And if we say 'A man could not imagine pain without having sometime felt it' – how do we know? How can it be decided whether it is true?

Part I, paragraph 315.

iii. Two pictures of a rose in the dark. One is quite black; for the rose is invisible. In the other, it is painted in full detail and surrounded by black. Is one of them right, the other wrong? Don't we talk of a white rose in the dark and of a red rose in the dark? And don't we say for all that that they can't be distinguished in the dark?

Part I, paragraph 515.

iv. Make the following experiment: *say* 'It's cold here' and *mean* 'It's warm here'. Can you do it? And what are you doing as you do it? And is there only one way of doing it?

Part I, paragraph 510.

11. *'Many masquerading as one'*

(*a*) A. N. Whitehead makes the point forcibly in his *Adventures of Ideas* (p. 221). He says:

Mr Joseph has been examining Mr W. E. Johnson's use of the term Proposition in his well-known Logical Treatise. Mr Joseph finds twenty distinct meanings. It is to be remembered that we are here referring to two of the most acute of modern logicians. Whether Mr Joseph has rightly interpreted Mr Johnson's phrases is not to the point. If Mr Joseph has found twenty distinct, though allied, meanings closely connected with the term Proposition, there are twenty such meanings, even though for the moment their divergencies may seem unimportant to Mr Johnson or to Mr Joseph. Importance depends on purpose and on point of view. So at any moment twenty new terms may be required by some advance in the subtlety of logical theory. Again, if Mr Johnson has employed twenty distinct meanings, it is because they were relevant to his argument, even though his argument may require further completion by reason of their un-noted distinction.

Do you agree that 'whether Mr Joseph has rightly interpreted Mr Johnson's phrases is not to the point'? Would the existence of twenty distinct meanings matter?

(b) Here is a passage from J. S. Mill about what he calls 'The Fallacy of Ambiguity', an error arising from the same word being used in different senses.

The following is a favourite argument of Plato. No one desires Evil knowing it to be so. To do wrong is evil; therefore no one desires to do wrong knowing that which he desires but only in consequence of ignorance. In this syllogism the ambiguous word is the middle term Evil, the double meaning of which is too obvious to need explanation: yet on this foundation Plato constructs his principal ethical doctrine in which he was followed by most of the philosophical sects among the later Greeks; that virtue is a branch of intelligence and is to be produced therefore mainly by intellectual cultivation. J. S. MILL, *A System of Logic*, p. 489.

What do you think is the double meaning of Evil, 'which is too obvious to need explanation'?

12. *'One masquerading as many'*

It may not always be obvious whether words or phrases connected by 'and' or 'or' or just with commas between them, stand for different things or the same thing. If the latter, they may be different aspects of the same entity or they may give more information about it.

At a very elementary level consider:

i. Do bring Esmeralda or Gladys to the party. (1 or 2?)
ii. I hope that Bertram, the next Chancellor of the Ex-

chequer, and the most intelligent man in the Cabinet will be there. (1, 2 or 3 ?)

At a more difficult abstract level consider the following extracts from the writings of Professor Gilbert Ryle. Do you think the nouns and adjectives separated by commas, 'and', 'or', stand for one or many ?

iii. Of course the standard theories of motives do not speak so crudely of qualms, pangs and flutters. They speak more sedately of desires, impulses or promptings. Now there are feelings of wanting, namely those we call 'hankerings', 'cravings' and 'itchings'. So let us put our question in this way. Is being interested in Symbólic Logic equivalent to being liable or prone to feel certain special hankerings, gnawings or cravings ? *The Concept of Mind*, p. 88.

iv. There are two quite different senses of 'emotions', in which we explain people's behaviour by reference to emotions. In the first sense we are referring to the motives or inclinations from which more or less intelligent actions are done. In the second sense we are referring to moods, including the agitations or perturbations of which some aimless movements are signs. In neither of these senses are we asserting or implying that the overt behaviour is the effect of a felt turbulence in the agent's stream of consciousness. In a third sense of 'emotion' pangs and twinges are feelings or emotions but they are not, save *per accidens*, things by reference to which we explain our behaviour. *The Concept of Mind*, p. 114.

13. The following extract from the works of the late J. L. Austin is an example of the very close analysis of words referred to in this chapter.

He is investigating the ways in which the verbs 'look', 'appear', 'seem' are used.

First, then, 'looks'. Here we have at least the following kinds of cases and constructions:

1. (a) It looks blue (round, angular, etc.).

   (b) He looks a gentleman (a tramp, a sport, a typical Englishman).

   (c) She looks *chic* (a fright, a regular frump).

Here we have the verb directly followed by an adjective or adjectival phrase.

2. (a) It [a colour] looks like blue [the colour].

   It looks like a recorder.

   (b) He looks like a gentleman (a sailor, a horse).

Here we have 'looks like' (cf. 'sounds like') followed by a noun.

3. (a) It looks as if $\left\{ \begin{array}{l} \text{it is} \\ \text{it were} \end{array} \right\}$ raining (empty, hollow).

   (b) He looks as if $\left\{ \begin{array}{l} \text{he is} \\ \text{he were} \end{array} \right\}$ sixty (going to faint).

4. (a) It looks as though we shan't be able to get in.

   (b) He looks as though he's worried about something.

Now let's try 'appears':

1. (a) It appears blue (upside down, elongated, etc.).

   (b) He appears a gentleman.

2. (a) It appears like blue.

   (b) He appears like a gentleman.

(It is very doubtful, though, whether this construction with 'appears' is really defensible; it certainly rings very dubiously to my ear.)

3 (and 4) (a) It appears as if (as though) . . .

         (b) He appears as if (as though) . . .

5. (a) It appears to expand.

   It appears to be a forgery.

   (b) He appears to like her (to have recovered his temper).

   He appears to be an Egyptian.

6. (a) It appears as a dark speck on the horizon.

   (b) He appears as a man of good character (*sc.* from this narrative. We can also say of an actor that he 'appeared as Napoleon').

7. It appears that they've all been eaten.

Notice particularly that here we have construction (viz. 5 – 7) which do *not* occur with 'looks'. These are in some ways the most important cases to attend to.

Of 'seems' we can say briefly that it shares the construction of 'appears' – though with fewer doubts about the propriety of (2). ('It seems like old times', 'It all seems like a nightmare') – *except* that 'seems' shows no construction analogous with (6), an important divergence.

Now how are we to tell the differences between these different words in these different constructions? Well, one difference certainly leaps to the eye: 'looks' is, to put it very roughly, restricted to the general sphere of *vision*, whereas the use of 'appears' or 'seems' does *not* require, or imply, the employment of any one of the senses in particular . . . .

But we must look, of course, for the minuter differences; and here we must look again at some more examples, asking ourselves in just what circumstances we would say which, and why.

Consider, then:

(1) He looks guilty.
(2) He appears guilty.
(3) He seems guilty.

> J. L. AUSTIN, *Sense and Sensibilia*, pp. 34–6.

The reader is now invited to consider for himself the 'minuter differences' between these three sentences.

Do you think that by analysis of this kind one finds out more about the facts or merely more about the words which are used to describe the facts?

Supplementary passages
A. 1. *On the 'Meanings' of words*

(1) From a Parliamentary report in *The Times* of 9 March 1961:

'. . . he [The Speaker] had to rule on what he conceived

to be the meanings of words, regardless of the intention of the person using them'.

(In the context it is in fact fairly clear that the Speaker is considering what people who heard the words would normally understand them to mean. It may well be thought that for parliamentary language this is a reasonable, and certainly the safest, course to take. The words were 'paid propagandist'.)

(2) Questions about precise 'meanings' of words are often raised in Law cases. The case considered here, reported in *The Times* of 24 May 1962, is particularly interesting because it raises the question of the 'meaning of meaning'.

The point at issue was whether the deaths of a man and his wife who were both killed at sea when the ship in which they were travelling in the South Pacific was lost without trace did or did not 'coincide'. Whether they did or not made a difference to the disposal of the estate.

The court ruled that their deaths did not coincide. In the course of a dissenting judgement the Master of the Rolls (Lord Denning) said:

So the critical question, raising a point of some importance in the interpretation of wills, was: what did the word 'coincide' mean in this will?

One way of approach much favoured in the nineteenth century was to ask what the ordinary and grammatical meaning was of the word 'coincide' as used in the English language. On that approach, the answer, it was said, was plain. It meant 'coincident in point of time'; and that meant, so it was said, the same as 'simultaneous' or 'at the same point of time'. So instead of interpreting the word 'coincide', one interpreted the word 'simultaneous'; and at that point came a difficulty, for no two people, strictly speaking, ever died at exactly the same point of time. In Hickman v. Pearcey ([1945] A.C. 304, at p. 345), Lord Simonds had said that 'proof of simultaneous death is impossible'. If, therefore, the word 'coincide' were given its ordinary and grammatical meaning, it would lead to an absurdity as meaning that the testator was providing in his will for an impossible event.

In order to avoid that absurdity, it was said that the word 'coincide' must be interpreted so as to mean death in such circumstances that the ordinary man would infer that death was simultaneous: and the argument proceeded to ask: When would an ordinary man say death was simultaneous? The answer was when two people were both blown to pieces at the same moment, such as by a bomb falling on the room in which they were sitting or by an aircraft in which they were travelling exploding in mid-air. The word 'coincide' was said to cover deaths so close together that there was no measurable period of time between them; it was also said that if the deaths were separated by any measurable interval, even by so much as a few seconds, they did not 'coincide'.

His Lordship had asked whether deaths were simultaneous when an aircraft crashed on a mountainside and all its occupants were killed. Counsel had said that they were not, for to be simultaneous there would have to be proof that they had died instantaneously at the same instant, and such proof would rarely be available. If ever there was an absurdity, that appeared to his Lordship to be one. It was said that when an aircraft exploded in mid-air, the deaths of the occupants coincided, but when it crashed into a mountainside they did not. The supporters of that argument invoked as their authority 'the ordinary man'. Such a man would, his Lordship thought, be amazed to find such a view attributed to him. Yet it was the argument which said that in this case the deaths of Dr Rowland and his wife did not coincide.

The fallacy of the argument seemed to his Lordship to be that it started from the wrong place. It proceeded on the assumption that, in construing a will, 'It is not what the testator meant, but what is the meaning of his words.' That might be the nineteenth-century view, but his Lordship believed it to be wrong and to have been the cause of many mistakes. The whole object of construing a will was to find out the testator's intentions in order to see that his property was disposed of in the way he wished. True, his intention must be discovered from the words he used; but there must be put on his words the meaning which they bore to him. To discover that meaning you would not get much help from the dictionary, for it was unlikely that the testator used a dictionary or the same dictionary as you. You should place yourself as far as possible in his position, taking note of the facts and circumstances known to him at the time, and then say what he meant by his words.

What did Dr Rowland and his wife mean by the word 'coincide' in their wills? When they came to make their wills it might be said: 'After all, one of those little ships might run on the rocks or something and we might both be drowned, or both killed in an aeroplane crash.' In those circumstances the husband would use the words 'coinciding with' not in the narrow meaning of 'simultaneous' but in the wider meaning of which they were capable, especially in this context, as denoting death on the same occasion by the same cause. It would not cross Dr Rowland's mind that anyone would think of such niceties as Mr Knox had presented to the Court. His Lordship declined to introduce such fine points into the construction of this will. He would hold that Dr Rowland when he made his will, intended the words 'coinciding with' to cover their dying together in just such a calamity as in fact happened, and that the Court should give his words the meaning which he plainly intended they should bear. He would have allowed the appeal.

[In opposing this view Lord Justice Harman said:]

Could these deaths on the evidence be held to have been simultaneous . . . ? His Lordship was satisfied that they could not. Not enough was known. It was not even known at what date, within a week, the ship went down nor was the whereabouts of either the testator or his wife at that time certain . . . the event was too uncertain to infer a simultaneous death . . . .

If that meaning of the word was out of the question, it was argued that 'coincident' in this will could mean 'at about the same time and as a result of the same catastrophe'. That was an impossible view. If it were in evidence that either survived the other, the will had provided for both events, and there was no warrant for introducing a reference to something other than time, namely the same catastrophe. The appeal should be dismissed.

[In agreeing with Lord Justice Harman, Lord Justice Russell said:]

... There was no evidence at all that the deaths were coincident in point of time in the mind of the ordinary man.

The suggestion had been made that this testator (in his particular armchair) had meant something wider, such as 'on the same occasion and by the same cause'; his employment in the Pacific would involve such perils or risks as might be inherent in travel between islands and atolls in small ships, therefore, this testator should be considered as having in mind just this kind of episode.

That appeared to his Lordship to be a wholly erroneous approach to the problem of construction. The question was: what events did the language in which the testator had expressed himself cover? To ask more was to desert the source from which his intention was to be gathered, his will as proved. His Lordship did not see why the testator in 1956, with the possibility of deaths coincident in time in England or elsewhere from accident by road or rail or air or by explosion, should be taken to have in mind, when using the phrase, deaths *not* coincident in time as a result of shipwreck in the Pacific.

The interesting point in all this from our point of view is the contrast between what the writer (in this case the testator) intended and what the 'words mean'.

Bewitchments

(3) A philosopher complains of bewitchment:

It is perfectly obvious that if I say 'I am thinking of a unicorn',

I am not saying both that there is a unicorn and that I am thinking of it, although, if I say 'I am hunting a lion', I am saying both that there is a lion, and that I am hunting it. In the former case, I am *not* asserting that the two properties, of being a unicorn and of being thought of by me both belong to one and the same thing; whereas, in the latter case, I am asserting that the two properties of being a lion and of being hunted by me *do* belong to one and the same thing. It is quite clear that there is *in fact*, this difference between the two propositions; although no trace of it appears in their verbal expression. And why we should use the same form of verbal expression to convey such different meanings is more than I can say. It seems to me very curious that language, in this, as in the other instance which we have just considered of 'Lions are real' and 'Lions are mammalian', should have grown up just as if it were expressly designed to mislead philosophers; and I do not know why it should have. Yet, it seems to me there is no doubt that in ever so many instances it has. G. E. MOORE, 'The Conception of Reality', from *Philosophical Studies*, pp, 216–17.

(4) An example where it is suggested that because the word exists some thing or entity may be thought to exist as well.

Suppose that I ask 'What is the point of doing so-and-so?' For example, I ask Old Father William 'What is the point of standing on one's head?' He replies in the way we know. Then I follow this up with 'What is the point of balancing an eel on the end of one's nose?' And he explains. Now suppose I ask my third question 'What is the point of doing *anything* – not anything *in particular*, but just *anything*?' Old Father William would no doubt kick me downstairs without the option. But lesser men, raising this same question and finding no answer, would very likely commit suicide or join the Church. (Luckily, in the case of 'What is the meaning of a word?' the effects are less serious, amounting only to the writing of books.) On the other hand, more adventurous intellects would no doubt take to asking 'What is the-point-of-doing-a-thing?' or 'What is the "point" of doing a thing?': and then later 'What is the-point-of-eating-suet?' and so on. Thus we should discover a whole new universe of a kind of entity called 'points', not previously suspected of existence. J. L. AUSTIN, *Philosophical Papers*, pp. 27, 28.

(5) Bergson cites another linguistic usage which may mislead:

If we look at it closely, we shall see that our habitual manner of speaking, which is fashioned after our habitual manner of thinking, leads us to actual logical deadlocks – deadlocks to which we allow ourselves to be led without anxiety, because we feel confusedly that we can always get out of them if we like: all that we have to do, in fact is to give up the cinematographical habits of our intellect. When we say 'The child becomes a man', let us take care not to fathom too deeply the literal meaning of the expression, or we shall find that, when we posit the subject 'child', the attribute 'man' does not yet apply to it, and that, when we express the attribute 'man', it applies no more to the subject 'child'. The reality, which is the *transition* from childhood to manhood, has slipped between our fingers. We have only the imaginary stops 'child' and 'man', and we are very near to saying that one of these stops *is* the other, just as the arrow of Zeno *is*, according to that philosopher at all the points of the course. The truth is that if language here were moulded on reality, we should not say 'The child becomes the man', but 'There is becoming from the child to the man'. In the first proposition, 'becomes' is a verb of indeterminate meaning, intended to mask the absurdity into which we fall when we attribute the state 'man' to the subject 'child'. It behaves in much the same way as the movement, always the same, of the cinematographical film, a movement hidden in the apparatus and whose function it is to superimpose the successive pictures on one another in order to imitate the movement of the real object. In the second proposition, 'becoming' is a subject. It comes to the front. It is the reality itself; childhood and manhood are then only possible stops, mere views of the mind; we now have to do with the objective movement itself, and no longer with its cinematographical imitation. But the first manner of expression is alone conformable to our habits of language. We must, in order to adopt the second, escape from the cinematographical mechanism of thought. . . .

No wonder, then, if philosophy at first recoiled before such an effort. The Greeks trusted to nature, trusted the natural propensity of the mind, trusted language above all, in so far as it naturally externalizes thought. Rather than lay blame on the attitude of thought and language toward the course of things, they preferred to pronounce the course of things itself to be wrong. HENRI BERGSON, *Creative Evolution*, pp. 329–31.

But it seems doubtful whether it would have occurred to them to 'lay blame on the attitude of thought and language'. Bergson went on to point out that since 'becoming' shocked the habits of thought and fitted ill into the moulds of language the Greeks declared it unreal. Reality for them was something which did not change.

(6) In a Supplement to *The Meaning of Meaning* about Language in the Study of Medicine, Dr F. G. Crookshank wrote:

Teachers of Medicine . . . seem to share the implied belief that all known, or knowable, clinical phenomena are resumable, and to be resumed, under a certain number of categories, or general references, as so many 'diseases': the true number of these categories, references, or 'diseases' being predetermined by the constitution of the universe at any given moment.

In fact, for these gentlemen, 'diseases' are Platonic realities. . . . This unavowed belief . . . carries with it the corollary that our notions concerning this, that, or the other disease are either

absolutely right or absolutely wrong, and are not merely matters
of mental convenience. In this way the diseases supposed to be
extant at any one moment are capable – so it is thought – of such
categorical exhaustion as are the indigenous fauna of the British
Isles and the population of London. That our grouping of like
cases as cases of the same disease is purely a matter of justification and convenience, liable at any moment to supersession or
adjustment, is nowhere admitted; and the hope is held out that
one day we shall know all the diseases that there 'are' and all
about them that is to be known. Op. cit., p. 342.

The attitude here complained of is almost certainly less
prevalent now than when it was written (*The Meaning of
Meaning* was first published in 1923), but it provides a good
example of the two errors of supposing (1) that because a
word exists a corresponding entity or thing therefore exists
as well; (2) that the clear-cut verbal classifications that we
make for convenience have necessarily corresponding to
them clear-cut divisions in the real world.

(7) Another example where it is suggested that the postula-
tion of a mysterious entity may have been a contributory
cause of fallacious thinking:

Physicists have been forced by their own data to a further
extension of the principles laid down in the seventeenth century
– namely that the business of science is the simple description
of observations, without postulating 'occult qualities', as
Newton called them, as the causes of the observations. . . . Take
the example of measuring. When I tell you that a stick is a foot
long, I am saying essentially that I have taken a standard object,
namely a foot rule, laid it alongside the stick, and found that
they match. But do I simply tell you that I have done this? No,
I say, 'The stick has a "length" of one foot.' I interpose the
occult quality, length, which I use as a model in my description
of what I did.

It has been a great part of Einstein's contribution to show that there is a great deal of harm in this, that in fact our talking about such entities as length and velocity and motion deceives us into ignoring certain fundamental features of our methods of observation . . . Einstein showed that the way to avoid all such difficulties is not to speak of length, at all, but always to describe simply and exactly what the observer does when he is measuring and then to try to work out simple relations between the observations. That is why his theory is called that of relativity. J. Z. YOUNG, *Doubt and Certainty in Science*, pp. 110–11.

(8) Later in the same book Professor Young suggests that the terminology of psychology consists partly of a series of 'occult qualities', similar to those to which Newton referred and similarly misleading.

They are models, if you like, used for convenience of description; we can do without them when we get better ones. Take the case of consciousness. In order to talk we postulate this entity as a kind of something within ourselves. 'But how can I doubt', you may say, 'that I have something called consciousness? I have consciousness and I may lose it when I bang my head.' But what is it that you really mean to say – that you lose it in the sense you lose a penny when it rolls under the sideboard? Of course not – what you meant to say was that following some particular blow on the back of your head you were unable to act as an observer or transmitter for ten minutes. 'Of course', you may reply, 'you can put it like that if you wish and I agree it tells you a little more detail but what else is gained by your new method? Is it not much easier and less clumsy to say "I lost consciousness"?' Surely the danger is that if we use these old methods we shall be misled into all the fallacies that would follow if we supposed consciousness to be a single thing which could exist independently of the rest of ourselves. Op. cit., pp. 155–6.

ON CONCEPTS

WE will examine now how the word 'concept' is used and what it is to handle one.

The word 'concept' is probably not used much today except in talking about philosophical or border-line philosophical questions. It is defined in the dictionary as a 'general notion', or the 'idea of a class of objects', but whereas the words 'idea' and 'notion' are frequently used in speaking and writing by people who would certainly not think of themselves as referring to a philosophical question, 'concept' tends to be a philosopher's word – it might be described in a derogatory way as an example of philosophical jargon. Professor Popper talks about '... those concepts (or notions or ideas)...' seeming to imply that he regards the three words as more or less synonymous. Examples of the use of the word in the writing of philosophers are legion. An exceedingly important recent philosophical work by Professor Gilbert Ryle is called *The Concept of Mind*. A recent inaugural lecture by Sir Isaiah Berlin was called *Two Concepts of Liberty*. It may help us to see just how they are using the word if we examine what it is that they are trying to do in these works.

Professor Ryle opens the Introduction to his book by saying:

This book offers what may with reservations be described as a theory of the mind. But it does not give new information about minds. ... The philosophical arguments which constitute this book are intended not to increase what we know about minds, but to rectify the logical geography of the knowledge we already possess.

The main theme of his book is the contention that the notion, or idea or concept of mind which most people, and even most philosophers, had hitherto accepted was an erroneous one, that it had been thought about in the wrong way, that in a sense 'mind' was a myth. He examines how the word is ordinarily used, the notion which it normally represents and claims to show that that notion is at least misleading.

In his *Two Concepts of Liberty* Berlin says: 'I do not propose to discuss either the history or the more than two hundred senses of this protean word recorded by historians of ideas. I propose to examine no more than two of these senses, but those central ones.' He calls these the notions of positive and negative freedom (a word which he uses as synonymous with liberty). These are described as 'The freedom which consists in being's one's own master and the freedom which consists in not being prevented from choosing as I do by other men.'

It is not relevant to our present purposes to examine these notions of freedom. What we are concerned with is to investigate what it is that is being done when one discusses 'concepts of liberty'.

Naturally Sir Isaiah Berlin makes many references to other philosophers who have written previously about liberty and related subjects. In particular he refers to the famous essay *On Liberty* by John Stuart Mill. It is natural to ask whether Berlin in writing about concepts of liberty envisaged himself as doing anything different in kind from what Mill did in writing *on* liberty. Could Professor Ryle's book equally well have been called 'On Mind'? Does this word 'concept', in fact, in the sort of contexts in which we are studying it perform any useful function at all? In this chapter we are considering the notion of concept and it might certainly have been entitled 'The concept of concept'. Might it equally well have been called 'On On'?

Let us consider – and this is often a profitable way of sorting out an entanglement – how this would apply in simpler cases. A book might be written entitled 'On the Internal Combustion Engine'. Could it equally well be called 'The concept of the Internal Combustion Engine'?

There would be no doubt in this case what the book was about. Any reader who started in ignorance would very soon have it dispelled. 'Internal combustion engine' is the general name for a class of concrete objects; there can be no doubt about the qualifications for membership of this class – they are indeed contained in the name – and no difficulty about what the words stand for. One would expect the book to tell how the internal combustion engine worked, perhaps also to inform us about its history – who made the first one when – and possibly give instructions as to how we could make one ourselves. There are two main and separate questions which we should expect the book to answer: the first is 'What *are* internal combustion engines? For what objects, things, ideas do the words stand?' The second is 'What are their qualities, characteristics, functions, history?'

The answer to the first question is short and simple because the words stand for a clearly defined class of physical objects. And when this question has been answered the notion or idea or concept of an internal combustion engine has really been explained. It would not be worth writing a book about it, though many books no doubt could be and have been written in answer to the second question.

The point is that there is only something which is

interesting, important and tricky to consider in the 'Concept of X', if X stands, not for a clear-cut class of material objects, but for an abstraction, a quality, something that cannot be pointed to and thus defined ostensively. What is normally being done in considering the concept of X is to analyse, examine, how the word X is used, what it is being used to stand for, and in doing this, if X is an abstraction, one must inevitably consider also the characteristics, qualities, of what it is being used to stand for; these are inevitably bound up with the criteria of what it is to be an X. If X stands for physical objects the two questions (What is an X? What are the qualities of an X?) are normally separable and to discuss or consider the concept of X is to answer only the first. Since this answer is short and simple it is not necessary to dignify the search by a high-sounding title such as 'discuss the concept'. If X stands for an abstraction the case is different.

To discuss the concept of brain is to come to an agreement as to how the word 'brain' is to be used, but since the word is already clearly defined discussion is hardly necessary. It is quite separate and easily seen to be separate from the consideration of how a brain functions, what it does.

To discuss the concept of mind is similarly to define how the word is used but this process is inextricably bound up with a consideration of the functions and qualities of mind. Similarly one cannot separate a consideration of what it is to which the word 'liberty' is applied from a consideration of what liberty is like, of what it is to be free.

It is because these processes are inevitably intertwined that the handling of concepts, the dealing with, understanding, and using of abstract words and ideas, is such a very tricky affair.

Let us take a trial run on a fairly simple example.

In a recent Scholarship General Paper at Oxford candidates were asked to 'examine the concept of loyalty'. We consider the sort of answer that might be given.

Everybody would have a rough general idea of how the word is used and to what it is normally applied. What we have to do is to examine this general usage and the ideas behind it rather more closely. In the first place it will probably be simpler and clearer if we take a look at the adjective 'loyal' rather than at the noun. The consideration of the abstract noun very often seems to remove the thought one degree further from reality. An adjective has to be applied, and to be thought of as applying, to some person or thing; whereas there is a danger that the abstract noun may be thought of as referring to some unattached, meta-phorically floating, entity. The adjective 'loyal' is normally applied to people. It is used to describe someone in his relationship to other people or to an institution. We talk of Smith being loyal to his friends, to his school or to his country, and it is this last use, the description of an attitude or a relationship to a sovereign or a country, which would probably spring first to the minds of most people. It is from this use that the others derive.

In thinking of loyalty to a sovereign one thinks also of the word 'allegiance', to which, interestingly, there is no corresponding adjective in current usage, though the adjective 'liege' does exist and may sometimes be em-ployed. Allegiance is probably associated for most people with vows made and promises given, with all the para-phernalia of knights and armour and feudalism. What are the characteristics of the relationship that is being described?

The promises and vows given would have been of devoted, unquestioning support in all circumstances. And those who would now be described as loyal to their king and country would have this adjective applied to them because it was thought that they would remain faithful, obedient, devoted, whatever the private character of the sovereign and however adverse the conditions. On the whole we probably only use the adjective 'loyal' about someone's personal relationships if we wish to imply that he will continue to be a devoted supporter when perhaps there might be some reason for withdrawing the support, when the object of devotion is being adversely criticized, when perhaps he or she has not been behaving very well.

We might describe this by saying that X is a very loyal person – he will stick to his friends through thick and thin. We would hardly call loyal a husband who is passionately devoted to his faithful, charming and universally popular wife because in a sense there is no occasion for loyalty, just as there is no occasion for courage unless a situation arises where there is danger or the possibility of danger. We might say that his loyalty had never been put to the test.

When we talk about someone being loyal to an institution other than a country (a loyal Yorkshireman, Conservative, member of the golf-club, old member of the school) we may not mean much more than that he goes back there often, subscribes to the relevant funds, has been a member for a long time, sends his sons there, as the case or cases may be; though there may also be the implication that he will stand up for the institution in the face of hostile criticism and perhaps that his support will be unquestioning.

In examining the concept of loyalty it would be relevant to point out that the adjective is almost invariably in fact used as one of commendation, though our examination may lead us to wonder whether approval is always the appropriate attitude. Loyalty in personal relationships may

involve allowing emotions of affection to outweigh reason;
perhaps it means standing up for X, making out the best
possible case for him, or by distortion or suppression a case
that is really better than the best that is honestly possible.
If this is so there may be an element of deception, of
oneself or of others. Or perhaps it means admitting that
X is wrong, has behaved badly, but deciding nevertheless to
remain his friend and supporter. Most people would
commend this, perhaps especially English people, for in this
country loyalty to a friend or colleague is generally highly
esteemed and may often be thought of as a more important
virtue than, say, speaking the truth or promoting the welfare
of the community. It might be generally agreed that as
with many similar questions it's a matter of degree; that if
one knows that one's colleague at the bank has committed a
brutal murder one should regard the protection of society
as more important than one's desire to be loyal. (In such a
dilemma it might be said that one is faced with a conflict of
loyalties, and in saying this the word 'loyalty' might be
used more widely to cover also one's duty to the community
as a whole.)

Loyalty in personal relationships is usually based on
personal affection. Loyalty to institutions may sometimes
be based on loyalty to an individual (e.g. a sovereign) or it
may be based on affection for a place, or a way of life, or on
pleasant memories and associations. There is a tendency in
such loyalties for the institutions to become personalized,
that is, thought of as supra-personalities who can be helped
or hindered, pleased or displeased, by one's actions. That
this way of thinking can be very dangerous is well exemplified by the growth of nationalistic feelings in this
century and the extent to which the loyal feeling 'my
country right or wrong' can lead to the condonation by

members of a State of tyrannical and wicked actions undertaken by their representatives. Loyalty to smaller institutions is less likely to lead to undesirable results, but if the support is blind, unquestioning, unreasonable, it is not easy to see on what grounds it is to be preferred to a line of action which is based on reason and, where necessary, criticism.

There are several points which arise from this analysis.

Firstly the question that is being considered, the investigation that is taking place, is not one which admits of a right answer or a precise conclusion. Many readers may disagree with what I have written; they may feel that I have been guilty of mis-statements or faults in emphasis. Further thought, further investigation in the shape of inquiries about the usages of other people, may support or may contradict their criticisms, but there does not exist any final, exact answer as to what is correct. There is the more correct and there is the less correct – to say, for example, that 'loyal to' is synonymous with 'fond of' would be to make a claim that is denied by the general practice of those who use the words; there is the completely incorrect – for example, to say that 'loyal to' is synonymous with 'opposed to'. But from the fact that in this matter there is a graduated scale from many quite wrong answers through a variety of more nearly correct answers, it does not follow that at the upper end of the scale there is a precise, correct solution. This follows inevitably and necessarily from the nature of the subject matter and is not merely due to the inadequacies of our tools, our methods of inquiry, or our mental shortcomings. The sands are shifting because it is in the nature of sands to shift.

What we are talking about is a complex of emotions, actions, motives, which vary from person to person; the language and the description are fuzzy and blurred because what is being referred to is fuzzy and blurred. There is no clear-cut concrete entity, no precise material thing.

Another reason why the sands inevitably shift is that in examining the concept of one elusive abstraction we are bound to use others. If I am explaining the construction and the working of a machine I will in the course of my explanation make plain, preferably by pointing or showing, exactly what I am using all the words to stand for. The demonstration and explanation of the constituent parts will inevitably enter into, or be a preliminary to, the explanation of the whole. One foot is placed firmly on the ground (no shifting sands here) before the next step forward is taken.

In examining the concept of loyalty, however, I may use many abstract adjectives or nouns – devotion, faithful, duty, for example. Clearly one might equally well have been asked to 'examine the concept' of any of these. Is one entitled to assume that these examinations have already been made, just as, if one is asked to write out the Theorem of Pythagoras in a geometry examination, one is entitled to assume as already proved the theorems which usually come before it? Again no shifting sand in geometry; brick is placed patiently on laborious brick and at the base there is a solid axiomatic foundation.

To ask this question is to expose again the difficulty of the treatment of abstract words. In examining the concept of loyalty I have assumed that the notions of faithfulness, duty, devotion are understood in a general way, just as if I were examining the concept of duty I might wish to assume that the concept of loyalty was vaguely understood. This procedure may appear rather hard to justify, unsystematic, irrational, unscientific, but the more one thinks about abstract words and their use the more one sees that no other procedure is possible. Inevitably, as modern philosophizing has been disparagingly called, it is 'talk about talk'. Any justification of the procedure must inevitably rest on the results. What, if anything, is gained by examining a concept? What, in particular, has been gained, or could be gained by anybody, by the examination of the concept of loyalty that has occupied the last few pages?

The claim would be that in spite of all the difficulties and drawbacks of the discussion one is led to see more clearly what is likely to be meant when someone is described as loyal, to understand more thoroughly the motives and emotions that inspire what is called loyalty and to be in a position to describe more accurately, though necessarily still very vaguely, and communicate more effectively, one's own thoughts on the subject. It would be claimed furthermore that not only are these things desirable in themselves, but also because the woolly, emotional lack of thought which so often accompanies writing and talking about abstractions can only too easily give rise to highly undesirable consequences in the future. It has certainly done so in the past.

Exercises

1. Examine the concepts of:

   i. Authority
   ii. Tolerance
   iii. Respectability
   iv. Orthodoxy

2. By being 'educated' I mean having such an apprehension of the contours of the map of what has been written in the past, as to see instinctively where everything belongs, and approxi-

mately where anything new is likely to belong; it means, furthermore, being able to allow for all the books one has not read and the things one does not understand – it means some understanding of one's own ignorance. T. S. ELIOT, quoted by F. R. Leavis, *The Common Pursuit*, p. 238.

Is this what you mean by being 'educated'? Discuss.

3. Referring to the cause of fires at a conference of chief fire officers, Mr Henry Brooke, then Home Secretary, was quoted as saying:

I cannot escape the conclusion that individual carelessness plays a large part. Carelessness is something of a cocktail: two parts ignorance, one part irresponsibility, with a dash of forgetfulness. *Daily Express*, 2 October 1963.

Discuss this analysis of carelessness.

4. 'Thank God I am not free, any more than a rooted tree is free.' D. H. LAWRENCE

Discuss the concept of freedom implicit in this.

5. 'The purpose of all educational institutions, public or private, is utilitarian and can never be anything else.' W. H. AUDEN

Discuss the way in which 'utilitarian' is used here.

6. Below is the first paragraph of a leading article in *The Times*, 4 September 1963.

Crossed Cultures

The concept of two cultures, one nurtured on science and the other on arts, was always an over-simplification. Interests are not determined wholly by education. School education at its worst is not utterly specialized. The interests of most of us are in part hybrid, as recent sample inquiries have shown. Moreover neither scientists nor the products of an arts education are all of a kind; and the kind of culture that education aims to produce is not the only one to be found in Britain. An anthropologist might recognize also a 'pop culture' – which at least is spontaneous; a 'suburban-materialist culture', not necessarily more given to thought; and no doubt others as well. The need to establish better communication between scientists and the rest of us is not one problem but several – a fact which the annual meeting of the British Association brings yearly to notice.

Discuss the way in which the writer seems to be using the word 'culture', and the concept of culture in general.

7. In his *Brave New World Revisited* Aldous Huxley suggests that a typical cry today of young people who think poorly of democracy may be: 'Give me television and hamburgers, but don't bother me with the responsibilities of liberty.' Op cit., p. 163.

Analyse the phrase 'the responsibilities of liberty'.

8. . . . these moderns take their stand on some unsolid subtleties, for they imagine that nothing is so perfect that there is not something more perfect, which is an error. (For example there is an infinity of regular figures, but one is the most perfect, namely the circle; if a triangle had to be made and there was no determination of the sort of triangle, God would assuredly make an equilateral triangle, because absolutely speaking, this is the most perfect.) G. W. LEIBNIZ, *Discourse on Metaphysics* (translation by P. G. Lucas and L. Grint), p. 6.

Do you agree that it is an error to suppose that 'nothing

is so perfect that there is not something more perfect'?
Discuss Leibniz's idea of 'perfection'.

9. ... to harness to its cart the strongest of all political motives,
the craving for freedom, socialism began increasingly to make
use of the promise of a 'new freedom'. The coming of socialism
was to be the leap from the realm of necessity to the realm of
freedom. It was to bring 'economic freedom', without which
the political freedom already gained was 'not worth having'.
Only socialism was capable of effecting the consummation of
the agelong struggle for freedom in which the attainment of
political freedom was but a first step.

The subtle change in meaning to which the word freedom
was subjected in order that this argument should sound
plausible is important. F. A. HAYEK, *The Road to Serfdom*,
p. 19.

Expound and explain what you think is 'the subtle change
in meaning' to which he refers.

10. Discuss the concept of Progress, with particular
reference to the following extracts from Herbert Spencer's
Essay on *Progress: its Law and Cause*.

Not only is the current conception of Progress more or less
vague, but it is in great measure erroneous. It takes in not so
much the reality of Progress as its accompaniments – not so
much the substance as the shadow. . . . Social progress is
supposed to consist in the produce of a greater quantity and
variety of the articles required for satisfying men's wants;
in the increasing security of person and property; in widening
freedom of action: whereas, rightly understood, social progress
consists in those changes of structure in the social organism
which have entailed these consequences.

. . . Only those changes are held to constitute progress which
directly or indirectly tend to heighten human happiness. And

they are thought to constitute progress simply *because* they tend to heighten human happiness. But rightly to understand progress, we must inquire what is the nature of these changes, considered apart from our interests. . . . Leaving out of sight concomitant and beneficial consequences, let us ask what Progress is in itself.

. . . It is settled beyond dispute that organic progress consists in a change from the homogeneous to the heterogeneous.

Now, we propose in the first place to show, that this law of organic progress is the law of all progress. Whether it be in the development of the Earth, in the development of Life upon its surface, in the development of Society, of Government, of Manufactures, of Commerce, of Language, Literature, Science, Art, this same evolution of the simple into the complex, through successive differentiations, holds throughout. From the earliest traceable cosmic changes down to the latest results of civilization, we shall find that the transformation of the homogeneous into the heterogeneous, is that in which Progress essentially consists.
HERBERT SPENCER, *Essays on Education etc.*, pp. 153-4.

ASKING THE RIGHT QUESTIONS

THE theme of this chapter is Russell's dictum, which we have already mentioned in Chapter 1, that the important thing in Philosophy is to ask the right questions. This is not only a matter of deciding what it is we want to know, but also of seeing what inquiries make sense, how the problems or the questions may most usefully be posed, whether there is some (metaphorical) territory which it is just not possible to explore. When philosophers have asked the same questions for thousands of years and have not only not succeeded in finding answers, but also seem to have come no nearer to finding them; when we see that in many cases they have not even reached agreement as to what sort of answers can be expected, what would count as an answer, it seems reasonable to suggest that perhaps it might be worth turning the spotlight on to the question and cease for the moment to wrestle with the task of trying to find a solution.

At the same time, however, it is foolish to suppose that the question can profitably be considered in complete isolation from the answer or possible answers. Indeed in order to come to a conclusion as to whether a question is satisfactory, one of the first things to be considered, the first question to ask ourselves about the question, is *how* to set about looking for an answer.

There is a very large number of questions for which the appropriate method is investigation, going and seeing. These are questions about the world around us and we set about answering them by looking at the facts of experience;

any answers that are produced should be empirically test-able. (What made my car stop? What will happen if I press that knob? How can cancer be cured?)

There are other questions which we will try to answer by a process of argument, deduction, putting together know-ledge we already possess. (What is 937 times 5642? How can I avoid being mated next move?)

There are also those questions which might be described as philosophical, and most people would probably try to answer them by just closing their eyes and thinking (or perhaps by just closing their eyes). Examples of such ques-tions are 'Are our wills free?', 'Must time come to an end?' It will be important in trying to decide whether these are satisfactory questions, to consider very carefully the most appropriate method for tackling them.

Before investigating what it is about questions that may make them unsatisfactory it will be useful to make two points about the kind of question to which the answer is empirically testable.

The first point is that though the question may be answerable in principle it may not be answerable in practice either now or ever. If I ask whether there are inhabitants of Mars no one on this earth now, as I write, can answer me with certainty, though it is perfectly possible that the question may be answerable by you as you read. There must *be* an answer and it seems reasonable to suppose that it will one day be found.

But consider the question 'How many people are there in Greater London now as I write at 12.50 on 15 August, 1961?' This is certainly answerable in principle. Provided that the boundaries of Greater London have been clearly defined there must be some definite number which is the answer. But I make bold to declare that it never will be answered in practice, that no human being does know or ever will know what the answer is.

The second point is that when we ask questions about matters of fact we normally know what *sort* of answers to expect, what sort of answer we would be prepared to accept.

If we ask what the other side of the moon looks like, the answer 'Like a Beethoven symphony' or 'Like the aroma of onions' would not be acceptable, would not count as an answer. Things can sound like that, or smell like that, but they can't *look* like that (though it may be argued that some highly imaginative people might say that listening to a Beethoven symphony or smelling onions conjures up a visual picture and *that's* what the other side of the moon looks like).

Or again we may make the same point by saying that in pursuing an investigation we must have some idea of what it is we are seeking, for the nature of what is being sought is likely to determine to some extent the method of investigation. If, as in Lewis Carroll's poem, it is a Snark that is being hunted, thimbles and hope may be appropriate: a nonsense hunt requires nonsense methods. Some people might suggest that metaphysical hunts in the past have sometimes had a snarkish flavour about them.

These two points that a question may be answerable in principle, but completely unanswerable in practice; and that it is important when asking a question to know the sort of answer that would be acceptable, are made most simply by considering trivial questions but will have important applications in more difficult abstract questions.

We come now to consider ways in which questions may be unsatisfactory, improper, wrong.

'VERBAL' QUESTIONS

There is first of all the question that looks like an inquiry about events in the real world, but which is seen on investigation and analysis to be merely an inquiry about how a certain word is to be used. If I ask, for example, whether a certain village is in Lancashire or in Yorkshire I am inquiring about a fact of which I am presumably in ignorance. I don't know exactly where the village is or I don't know exactly where the dividing line between Lancashire and Yorkshire is. If, however, I want to know whether Gubbins who was born in Lancashire and has spent most of his life in Yorkshire is a Lancastrian or a Yorkshireman, I am aware of the geographical and biographical facts but want to know how the words 'Lancastrian' and 'Yorkshireman' are to be used, which label is to be attached.

Someone might answer my query by saying that it all depends on what I mean by 'Lancastrian', and he would of course be perfectly right. But whether a question is a fact-finding one or a verbal one, whether it is to be answered by empirical investigation or by deciding what is the most generally accepted or convenient way of describing agreed facts, depends on the context and the circumstances. To any question that could ever be asked it would always be relevant to say 'It all depends what you mean by . . .' but if the words under consideration are unambiguous and are generally used to mean the same thing it would be a rather foolish and irritating remark. Questions about clear-cut concrete entities, are obviously much less likely to be 'verbal' than questions about abstractions, though there may still be doubt as to precisely how the terms are to be defined. If I ask how many marbles there are in this bag there can be no

doubt about what I want to know or how to set about finding
the answer. But if I ask how far it is from Gloucester to
Cambridge the answer I want and the definition of the terms
would depend on my purpose in asking the question. Do I
want to know the approximate distance by road because
I want to drive there, or in a straight line because I want to
fly there? Or do I want, for some other purpose, a more
accurate estimate of the distance? In which case 'Gloucester' and 'Cambridge' must be more precisely defined.

If, however, the question is asked 'Are kind people
generous?' it is probable that the questioner merely wants
guidance as to how the words 'kind' and 'generous' are to
be used. It is unlikely that anyone would set about answering this question by investigating the generosity of those to
whom a metaphorical label 'kind' is already attached.

We must not suppose that there is anything necessarily
'wrong' about verbal questions; the facts about how words
are to be used may be as important and necessary to
investigate as any others. The question only becomes
unsatisfactory or misleading when it is thought to be of one
kind – designed to find out facts other than verbal facts – but
proves on investigation to be merely verbal. It is certainly
not the case, however, that questions can be simply divided
into fact-finding ones and verbal ones. As we have already
suggested it depends on the circumstances. What does the
inquirer want to know, and for what purpose? Is he in
search of some facts or is he merely concerned about how to
describe them?

'MERELY' VERBAL

We must be careful, however, not to assume that how we
describe them is unimportant. It is certainly true that

people may make mistakes by erroneously supposing that they are investigating an important issue when they are in fact only inquiring how a word has been, is, or is to be, used. And it is especially the case that a great many inconclusive arguments are seen on analysis to be merely verbal. The 'merely', however, needs a great deal of watching, it may matter very much which label is applied.

Suppose for example that Perewinkle is on trial in a court of law. Was his course of action legal or illegal? Very often, obviously, the dispute or argument will be about the facts of the case, but let us suppose that there is no dispute about the facts, that both sides are agreed about what happened. The dispute is about whether what he did was or was not illegal, whether his course of action does or does not fall within such and such a description.

Those whose task it is to resolve this dispute must perhaps try to interpret the intention of those who framed the laws, and they must perhaps refer to previous interpretations as laid down in case law. It can certainly be argued that what is being decided is whether to attach the label 'legal' or 'illegal' to Perewinkle's action, but as the labels also have written on them 'to go free' and 'to go to prison' Perewinkle might be excused for objecting to a description of the dispute as 'merely verbal'. Labels do matter; it makes a difference whether they say 'to be hanged' or 'to go free', or '6d.' or '£600', or 'To Tooting' or 'To Timbuctoo'.

The point is of course that labels may merely give names or they may give instructions, or they may, and this is where the muddle may arise, give a name which implies or involves instructions or consequences. In deciding whether to attach the label 'illegal' to a certain course of action we are deciding whether that action is sufficiently against the interests of the community to merit punishment. To say that

we are deciding how to use the words 'legal' or 'illegal' is
in a sense true but can be seriously misleading. To describe
a question or a dispute as *merely* verbal is a reasonable thing
to do only when it can be seen that we are asking what
name to attach to a certain thing or idea or course of action,
and that no further consequences follow from attaching or
not attaching the name; when it really does not matter
which we call it. To ask, for example, whether Coote is bald
when he stands in front of us and there is no doubt about
how much hair he has, is to make an inquiry about how the
normally loose word 'bald' is to be used, and provided that
there are no further implications or consequences, that it is
not, for example, illegal for bald men to bathe in the sea on
the sabbath, it would be reasonable to describe it as a merely
verbal question and it is desirable that it should be seen as
such. But to ask whether my Dutch friend, Hadter, is sane
would be a very different matter.

It will be interesting to consider for a moment a more
difficult question still. Suppose I am wondering not
whether Perewinkle's action was legal, but whether it was
right. I know precisely, not only just what he did but also
the circumstances in which he did it and the resulting consequences. He has told me, and I have no reason to
disbelieve him, just what his motives were. In other words
there is no doubt about the facts, about what happened, the
question is how to describe them.

In the question about the legality of the action there does
at least purport to be a set of criteria for deciding, though it
may be difficult to judge whether these criteria apply. But in
the question about the rightness of the action the criteria are
usually less generally agreed and less clearly laid down. It is
certainly less likely than in the questions of legality that the
answer will have important consequences for Perewinkle or

for anybody else. In a sense it might be described as a
'verbal' question but it is one that necessitates the examination of the concept of right and of morality in general.
Beyond remarking that this is a very difficult matter we will
not pursue it further now.

The important points that emerge from this discussion of
verbal questions are firstly that we must not be deluded into
thinking that we are inquiring about the facts if we are only
asking how we shall describe them; and secondly that this
decision as to how they shall be described may or may not
be important; for certain purposes and in certain contexts
the decision whether the facts fit some criteria or accord
with some concept may matter very much.

QUESTIONS THAT SUGGEST THE ANSWERS

We consider now another set of unsatisfactory questions,
namely those questions which are phrased in such a way that
they suggest the answers which are expected, or hoped for,
or required. It might be said that in a sense the answers are
'built-in' to the questions.

Objections are sometimes made against a counsel in a
court of law that he has asked a 'leading question', prompt-
ing the answer that is desired. A schoolmaster may sometimes do it, kindly, in the class-room when he has abandoned
hope of getting the right answer any other way.

A question, especially one about a matter of opinion,
may also be phrased in such a way as to indicate the attitude
of the questioner and his expectation that others will agree
with him. Such a question is often called 'loaded'. 'Do you
approve of the suggested betrayal of the Commonwealth?'
would be a loaded way of asking someone whether he was
in favour of the United Kingdom joining the Common

Market. It is also possible to impose limits on the scope of answers by making the questions 'closed' rather than 'open'. 'Do you intend to vote Conservative or Liberal in the next election?' is a closed question, of which the open version would be simply 'For whom, if anyone, do you intend to vote?' If the alternatives mentioned in a 'closed' question exhaust all the relevant possibilities it becomes, of course, equivalent to an open question.

In an age when sociological investigation in the form of Gallup Polls is becoming more and more of a science the precise phrasing of a question so that it shall not be loaded or leading or improperly closed assumes considerable importance. But it is, on the whole, for particular acts of questioning about practical affairs rather than for more general investigations of a philosophical nature that questions are likely to be unsatisfactory in this way. Questions that are leading or loaded are usually so by the intention of the questioner in the particular circumstances. He who asks is generally aware, to some extent at least, of the suggestive nature of what he is doing. A kind of error that is linked with this, but which is much more likely to be perpetrated unconsciously and to be found in questions about abstract matters, is the error that arises from what might be called the 'built-in assumptions' of the question.

BUILT-IN ASSUMPTIONS

This type of unsatisfactory or improper question is of frequent occurrence and is particularly dangerous and misleading. It is exemplified at a very elementary level by the well-known stock question 'Have you stopped beating your wife?' Notice that under certain circumstances this can be a perfectly satisfactory and proper question. If I who ask am well aware that my Italian acquaintance, Wacca, of whom I make the inquiry, has been in the habit of beating his wife, there is nothing wrong with this question except that it might be rather tactless. It is only an improper question if the assumption made is not true, or if at any rate it is not legitimate to make it; if it is not an agreed premiss from which questioner and questioned can start.

The questions that make illegitimate or erroneous assumptions, the questions that beg the question, form perhaps one of the most frequent and fruitful sources of error in the whole history of philosophy. The error stems above all from a failure to rid oneself of preconceived notions. As one grows up one absorbs in the processes of one's education and learns to some extent unconsciously a whole set of ways of thinking about life, about the physical world, and about the various subjects which one studies. These may be unquestioningly taken for granted to an extent that is difficult to realize without a considerable effort of reflection. In order to make important new steps forward in thinking it is necessary to break away from the generally accepted notions, from what Professor J. K. Galbraith has called in the sphere of Economics 'The conventional wisdom'. It is interesting that in two books which may well come to be regarded as among the most important of the first half of the twentieth century, *The General Theory of Employment, Interest and Money* by J. M. Keynes and *The Concept of Mind* by Professor Ryle, the authors have both made this point in their introductions.

Keynes says:

The composition of this book has been for the author a long struggle to escape, and so must the reading of it be for most

readers if the author's assault upon them is to be successful –
a struggle of escape from habitual modes of thought and
expression. The ideas which are here expressed so laboriously
are extremely simple and should be obvious. The difficulty
lies, not in the new ideas, but in escaping from the old ones,
which ramify, for those brought up as most of us have been,
into every corner of our minds.

And Ryle says:

Some readers may think that my tone of voice in this book
is excessively polemical. It may comfort them to know that the
assumptions against which I exhibit most heat are assumptions
of which I myself have been a victim. Primarily I am trying
to get some disorders out of my own system.

Progress was not made with the problems with which
they were wrestling until they were restated, until the
questions were phrased in a different way, until a break was
made with the old question-begging form of the question
or the problem.

Perhaps the point will be made most effectively by
considering some examples at various levels of subtlety and
difficulty and in various subjects.

Almost any question that is asked or problem that is
stated is bound to assume something. In our everyday
living and in our ordinary conversations these assumptions
will usually be commonly held and generally agreed, though
it may none the less be useful occasionally to subject them
to scrutiny. Assumptions that are erroneous may sometimes
be the source of embarrassment, as when the present
writer was asked after walking up a hill in Wales: 'Where
have you done most of your mountaineering?' In our
ordinary social intercourse we have all of us asked or been
asked questions which make assumptions of a rude or of a

flattering nature. 'What colour is your other frock?' 'What make is your other car?' 'What were your dates at the University?' 'Who is your favourite Romantic poet?'

These questions may very often not be intended and not be taken seriously; and obviously an assumption that is flattering in one context to one person (that you have *another* car) may be the reverse to someone else (that you only have *one* other car). Most people have probably at some time committed the error of failing to point out immediately that a flattering assumption was false and have regretted it afterwards.

When the erroneous assumptions are matters of fact then, although they may not always be discovered, they are usually in principle easily discoverable. It is when the errors are bound up with abstract concepts that they are likely to remain undetected and may cause serious mistakes in our thinking. What is happening is usually that it is being taken for granted that the concept is of a certain kind when it is at least open to doubt and discussion whether this is so. In a sense the question is being 'closed' by the illicit assumptions that are built in, and it would of course always be possible to open it by rephrasing.

Here is an example from economics.

For a long time the early economists were much concerned with the question of value. Two closely related questions that were asked were 'What is this object *really* worth?' and 'What is it that determines the real worth or value of an object?' Many different answers were given to the second question; Marx said that the value of an object depended upon the amount of human labour put into its construction, others stressed the magnitude of the need which the object satisfied. But no satisfactory solution was produced, it appeared an insoluble problem. As indeed it was, but the reason for its insolubility lay in the fact that it was a pseudo-problem, that the wrong question was being asked. And what was wrong with the question was the assumption that there was such a thing as real or intrinsic value, or that the concept of 'intrinsic value' was useful or intelligible. While the reality and intelligibility of 'intrinsic value' were assumed the question as to what determined it appeared an interesting but a tough and intractable problem, about which many experts wrote many thousands of words. As soon, however, as the spotlight is turned on the question, on the assumption that is being made, the difficulties fade away. What is meant, what can be meant, by the concept of real value? One can talk about the value which an object has in exchange, the price which it will fetch, and this price will obviously be different at different times and in different places, and will depend on a whole lot of circumstances. One can also talk about the subjective estimate of value that different people put on it, where they place it on their scale of preferences, and this again will clearly vary from person to person and for the same person at different times. But the concept of intrinsic, absolute value is seen to be useless, misleading and based on a myth. The mistake arises basically from supposing that what is really relative is in some sense absolute. A similar mistake is to be found in another subject, mechanics.

If we ask how fast a body is travelling the assumption in most contexts would be that we want to know its speed relative to the earth. The discovery in the study of elementary mechanics that the earth is moving relative to other planets often prompts the question as to how fast this body is *really* travelling, not relatively but really. To ask this question would be to assume that there is such a thing as absolute velocity and would be to misunderstand the nature of the concept of velocity which it is easily seen can only be relative. The realization that 'absolute velocity' is a myth and that only relative velocity has any meaning may help us to understand the necessary relativity of other things.

A similar assumption that is often built-in to a question is that there exists an absolute, correct solution to a problem when in fact it may well be the case that the answer can only be conditional, in a sense relative, perhaps a matter of opinion. 'What is the right way of doing this?' *may* have a unique correct answer, for example if 'doing this' is fitting the last piece into the jig-saw puzzle where what is correct is defined by those who constructed the puzzle. But if 'doing this' is putting on my tie, or playing a stroke at cricket, or schooling a horse, or bringing up the young, the answer is that it all depends. It depends on what one wants, one's purpose, one's tastes. Some methods have been found by the test of experience to be sometimes or even usually more effective than others and it would be reasonable to describe them as 'better', but a request for *the* right way makes an assumption that is very often false, though 'right' ways can always be defined for particular purposes. A more important example of this same assumption is to suppose that in any moral problem there is always a uniquely *right* course of action. Considerable differences of opinion exist as to whether this is so or not, but whatever the truth of the matter it is certainly wise to notice when this assumption is being made and to be aware of the fact that it is one that can be and often is criticized.

Closely allied with the assumption of the unique solution, the right course of action, is the assumption that qualities can be measured, especially the very vague, overall, portmanteau quality of being 'better than'. 'Which is the better game, football or cricket?' 'Who is the better man, Brown or Green?' It all depends. Better for what, from what point of view? What is it exactly that the questioner wants to *know*? An analysis and a cross-examination of the questioner may lead to a rephrasing of the question that will make it less unsatisfactory. If games or people or anything else are to be graded, criteria for the grading must be stated. It is possible that these criteria may be implicit in the context of the question, but it is possible also that even if they are in some sense there they will prove to be insufficient. We must be careful not to assume that all qualities are capable of being measured and graded, many of them are much too indefinite and relative. We shall have more to say about this in the chapter on Value Judgements.

Another illegitimate assumption that may be made about concepts is to suppose that concept X is applicable to concept Y when this is not certainly so. An example at a trivial level which may bring out the point obviously, would be to ask whether wasps or flies are more generous. The concept of generosity, though necessarily vague, is in general intelligible and sensible, but we do not normally suppose that it makes sense to talk as though it were applicable to wasps or flies, though it is perfectly possible that some people might claim that the concept was applicable to their domestic pets.

Similarly the assumption might be made that moral concepts are applicable to groups such as states, corporations, banks, schools. It would clearly be rash to do this without some analysis of the concept of a group personality (see page 104 for discussion of this point). Assumptions, which may be erroneous, about the nature of a concept are, also responsible for a type of unsatisfactory or misleading question which requires particularly careful handling – the type that takes for granted a categorization of Reality of a certain kind. An obvious example is the question that Philosophers have asked for thousands of years, 'How do mind and body interact?' It might be thought that the assumption that is being made of the division of a human personality into mind and body was an obvious and reasonable one, but as has already been mentioned it is one that has recently been much questioned, notably by Professor Gilbert Ryle in *The Concept of Mind*. This categorization assumes that the mind and the brain are two distinct entities, but to make the assumption, or indeed to make the contrary assumption that they are only one entity, may be a misleading thing to do. Perhaps a clearer way of looking at it may be that whether we think of the mind and brain as one or two should depend on the context, on the purpose for which we are considering them.

There are a whole host of questions and investigations in different subjects that take for granted various categories. Economists may ask questions about relationships between the various factors of production. Philosophers and to some extent Psychologists in the past have asked questions about the Will, the Reason, the Emotions. The categorization of reality that such questions imply may truly correspond with the facts, the distinctions that are being made may represent the most convenient and intelligible way of thinking about these matters. We must be careful, however, not to regard the distinctions as separations,[1] to remember that the categorization has been undertaken by man for certain purposes and that it may be a fruitful and helpful start to one's investigation to scrutinize it carefully.

1. 'One of the perennial curses of thought is the making separate of what is only distinguishable.' L. A. REID, *Philosophy and Education*, p. 82.

BUILT-IN UNANSWERABILITY

The questions that we have been considering are rendered at least unsatisfactory by their built-in assumptions. In some of the more extreme cases it might be argued that they are rendered unanswerable, or at least only answerable after sorting out and rephrasing. We consider now the most extreme cases of all in which the unanswerability is logically built in.

The most obvious examples are in a sense 'trick' questions, like the well-known one 'Is the statement "this statement is false" true or false?' If one answers 'true', then it is false; and if one answers 'false', then it is true. The fact that it is unanswerable need cause no particular concern; the puzzle arises from the fact that as with many similarly puzzling statements it is self-referring. Such questions and statements are similar to investigations which are self-defeating and tasks which are logically impossible. Some specimens of each may help to elucidate the point.

An investigation that is self-defeating is one in which the act of investigation necessarily removes or obscures that which is being investigated. It is like a dog chasing its shadow, or a man trying to look (without the aid of mirrors) at the back of his own head: the act of pursuit removes that which is being pursued, the act of looking removes that which one wants to see. It might be said that the attempt to see ourselves as others see us, is similarly self-defeating. In the literal, physical sense of 'see' it obviously is, but it will also be true in the sense of trying to see our character objectively as it appears to other people, for the act of putting ourselves metaphorically in their shoes will alter just that very character that we are trying to examine. It is analogous to Heisenberg's Uncertainty Principle that the act of measuring alters that which is being measured and that which is measuring.

Seeing ourselves as others see us might be said to be both a physical and a logical impossibility. Here is another example of a task which is both. Suppose that I have in front of me on the table a collection of small orange and green objects and two large boxes, one orange, one green. My instructions are to put all the orange things in the green box and all the green things in the orange box. Obviously all is plain sailing until the final moment of agonizing difficulty, which may be physical or mental according to my temperament and intelligence, when I either try simultaneously to put the orange box in the green and the green box in the orange or I sit back and try to solve the problem by thinking. This is an absurd example but it sometimes happens in important ways that mankind seem to set themselves tasks which are logically impossible, as when all nations simultaneously try to achieve a favourable balance of trade.

Questions that are logically unanswerable will often be trivially and obviously so. If I ask 'What does an invisible man look like?' or 'How can one get to know the unknowable?' or 'How does one answer an unanswerable question?' it is quite clear in each case that the question excludes the possibility of an answer. There is no difficulty about this and it may be wondered why it should be thought worthwhile to mention such questions. The point is that this type of unanswerability may be concealed and not laid bare, and that necessarily fruitless attempts may be made to answer questions in which there is a similar, but subtly hidden, built-in logical unanswerability. And this may be connected with the rejection of certain types of answer, the refusal to allow them to count as answers.

Suppose for example that someone asks 'What is Reality really like?' What sort of answer would be admissible? Does he want to know what Reality really *looks* like, or *smells* like or *sounds* like? And if as is likely he rejects these and says that he wants to know what Reality really *is* like, what does he mean, what *can* he mean by that? We might make the same point by saying that no answer that could be given is empirically verifiable, for how can one discover whether that *is* what Reality is really like?

What is being suggested is that such a question may be made logically unanswerable in part by the attitude of the questioner to answers that are suggested. We shall have more to say about this particular question later when we come to examine the concept of Reality.

The errors that we have been describing in the asking of questions may obviously also be made in the giving of answers. Especially is it true in philosophizing that a perfectly proper question may be answered in a form that begs the question, that makes, for example, just that very assumption that the question is designed to test. This is obviously most likely to be true when we question the assumptions that are most firmly embedded in our ways of thinking and talking. We have in this chapter put the spotlight on the question, on the statement of the problem, for the simple reason that both in logic and in time it must come first. But, as we have suggested, it would be a great mistake to try to consider it in isolation from the answer and especially from the possible methods of trying to find the answer, to solve the problem. We have tried to show some of the ways in which questions may be wrong or unsatisfactory. Clearly, however, their inadequacy or their wrongness may be a matter of dispute. And what we must try to do is to think what it is that the questioner wants to know: if we can discover this, even though perhaps only vaguely, it may be possible by a rephrasing of the question to lay bare or to remove the implicit assumptions and make it intelligible and answerable.

Consider, for example, the question 'Which is the more aggressive, the USA or the USSR?'

This is not obviously a silly or an unanswerable question and it is one which a very large number of people, especially most of the inhabitants of the USA and the USSR, would answer without any hesitation. But it is certainly a question which requires careful analysis and examination and to which the unhesitating answer would be likely to be merely the emotional expression of an attitude.

There is first of all the very difficult matter as to what we mean by ascribing a personal quality (that is, one which is normally attributed to persons) to a corporate, collective noun or phrase such as the USSR. The name of a country or a corporation or a group obviously requires careful handling and can mean quite different things in different contexts. If I say, 'England is beautiful' I refer to the country or the buildings; if I say 'England is good at cricket' I refer to some selected few of her inhabitants, or possibly to some sort of imagined average standard of merit of all her inhabitants; if I talk about 'Perfidious Albion' I would probably be thinking of her statesmen though I might be referring to her inhabitants in general. To talk about a country being aggressive would be most likely to mean that her policy or behaviour towards other nations might lead to war, though in some contexts it might mean that to pick quarrels was a national trait, a general, frequently found characteristic of the individuals who made up the nation.

The point is that in attempting to answer such a question it must be examined, tidied up, analysed, before it can be usefully discussed, or, in a sense, in the process of discussing it. And it may well be said that it would be difficult or impossible to ask this question or pose this problem briefly, without making assumptions that need to be examined or without leaving obscure points which require clarification.

It might in fact be claimed by the questioner, if he is criticized, that it is precisely this reformulation of the question in clearer and necessarily lengthier terms that he is demanding.

Exercises

1. Consider whether the following questions are answerable (*a*) in principle, (*b*) in practice.

i. What was the average age of present Members of Parliament two years ago?

ii. What was the average weight of present Members of Parliament two years ago?

iii. How does the value of a pound now compare with its value 300 years ago?

iv. What is the whole truth about John Jones?

v. What is the whole truth about what happened in this room yesterday?

vi. How many times does the sequence 12345 occur in the development of π?

2. Might the following questions be described in some contexts as merely verbal? In what sort of contexts? Discuss:

i. Is that what you call aquamarine?

ii. Is that what you call being responsible?

iii. Is Economics a science?

iv. Is unreasonable behaviour the same as irrational behaviour?

v. Can a person be wise but not intelligent?

vi. Are we ever really free?

vii. Would you say that conceited people were happy?

viii. What is meant by calling a work of art 'inspired'?

ix. What is the difference between a Rolls-Royce and a Jaguar?

x. What is the difference between banter and badinage?

xi. What is the difference between poetry and prose?

xii. What is the meaning of life?

3. Consider the kind of answers that would be acceptable to the following questions. What sort of things are the questioners likely to be trying to find out?

i. Why have no animals got three legs?

ii. Why is Monday washing-day?

iii. Why did you punish him?

iv. Why should we keep our promises?

v. What is the meaning of this disgraceful behaviour?

vi. 'Why are we weighed upon with heaviness,
   And utterly consumed with sharp distress,
   While all things else have rest from weariness?
   All things have rest; why should we toil alone...?'
                    (TENNYSON, *The Lotus-Eaters*)

vii. Why hasn't the car been put away?

viii. Why don't you stop asking people these silly questions?

4. Discuss the extent to which the following questions might be regarded as loaded or leading:

i. Are you in favour of all this doctrinaire egalitarianism?

ii. Do you think that in broadcasts to Russia we should say something about our point of view as well as giving the news?

iii. Do you think that the broadcasts to Russia should include propaganda as well as news?

iv. 'Why should manufacturers sweat to sell abroad if their earnings are frittered away on foreign food?' GERALD NABARRO, M.P., as reported in the *Daily Express*, 3 August 1961.

v. Do you think that these materialistic times are to be preferred to the more leisured age of the past?

5. Consider the built-in assumptions, if any, of the following questions:

i. Is he one of us?

ii. How are past experiences stored in the mind?

iii. Which is the most wicked – envy, hatred or malice?

6. Do you think the following questions need reformulating or tidying up? Discuss how this might be done:

i. Are women better housewives than they used to be?

ii. Which is the more truly educated man – the classic or the scientist?

iii. What is the most significant cultural activity?

iv. Are all men brothers?

v. Which is more important – Justice or Freedom?

7. Comment on the following questions:
(e.g. Are they likely to be just verbal? Do they want sorting out? What sort of answer might be given? etc.)

i. How can we leave the present moment?

ii. Can a computer think?

iii. Is it wicked to be stupid?

iv. Is a man going up a moving staircase, which is moving down faster than he is moving up, going upstairs or downstairs?

v. Where is the image in the mirror?

vi. What is a number?

vii. 'If from one day to the next you promise: "Tomorrow I will come and see you" – are you saying the same thing every day, or every day something different?' L. WITTGENSTEIN, *Philosophical Investigations*, paragraph 226

VALUE JUDGEMENTS

IN our everyday life we are commonly making comparisons between things and between people. What are being compared and the qualities in respect of which they are being compared will differ widely, as will also the reasons why it may be thought interesting or useful to make the comparisons. In this chapter we are going to try to analyse and examine comparisons in general, and in particular the whole set of comparisons or implicit comparisons which are called value judgements. We shall be concerned here only with those statements which are about the world of experience, not with statements such as those of pure mathematics which, if true, are necessarily so.

We start by considering two examples, one at each end of a rather important scale.

'OBJECTIVE' COMPARISONS

I have in front of me two sticks, and I say that this one (A) is longer than that one (B). It would be generally agreed that whether this is true or not is a matter of fact. The statement can be subjected to a public test by putting them beside one another, and, supposing for the moment that the difference is obvious to the naked eye and that we are not entertaining eccentric metaphysical notions about the nature of reality, there would be no difficulty in coming to an agreed decision about it provided that all observers understood the meaning of the phrase 'longer than'. It might happen, however, that to the naked eye the two sticks appeared to be about the same length. One person might then say that he thinks A is longer, while someone else thinks B is. A scientist with instruments for measuring accurately might then be called in to decide between them. Although the two observers have formed different views about the comparative lengths of the stick, they would both be likely to agree that it is nevertheless true that which is the longer is a matter of fact and not of opinion, that one of them is right and the other wrong. The scientist may give them the answer that to the degree of accuracy to which his instruments are capable of measuring he cannot separate them, but it would still be regarded as likely that with more accurate instruments he would be able to, and even if he couldn't their comparative length remains a matter of fact, though the facts may be difficult to discover.

Suppose again that A and B are made of different materials, that their lengths are very nearly the same and it is found that owing to expansion in the heat A is longer at certain high temperatures and B is longer at low temperatures, which then is *really* longer? It is not hard to see that this would be a silly question. The facts are as they are; the one is longer at some temperatures, the other at others. If it were thought to be convenient 'real' length could be defined as length at a certain temperature, and in that case the question would be made an answerable one, but that would probably seem to most people rather an artificial thing to do. This comparison of length is a matter of fact which may be subjected to a public, scientific test. Any statement that is made about it can be, at least in principle, verified or falsified, though there may be particular circumstances making a verification or falsification difficult. Such a statement, one that is a matter of fact, capable of public testing, that can be verified or falsified by experience (empirically), is often called *objective*. It is easy to think of whole classes of comparisons of a similar kind, public statements about the physical material world, where there is no difficulty in theory about discovering the facts, and no difficulty about describing them in such a way as to inform other people effectively what the facts are.

'SUBJECTIVE' COMPARISONS

We now come to our second example. Suppose that someone tries out two chairs by sitting in each of them one after the other and then says: 'This chair is more comfortable than that.' It is probable that if questioned he would agree that what he really means is that he personally finds the one chair more comfortable than the other, with perhaps the implication that most other people are likely to do so too. In other words although the statement may appear at first to be of the same kind as 'this chair is heavier than that', it becomes clear as soon as we think about it that the speaker is likely to be expressing or perhaps describing his own attitude to the chair, though what he says may be influenced by what he thinks are the likely attitudes of other people. Statements which express the attitude of the speaker are often called *subjective*.

The distinction which we have just implied between *expressing* an attitude and *describing* is not always easy to make in practice though it is useful and quite simple to see the difference in principle. If as I sink into a chair I utter a few simple words of delight I am probably *expressing* an attitude; if I say to my guest 'I find this chair more comfortable than that' I am merely describing one. Clearly we often make statements which do both.

There may sometimes be arguments about the comparative comfort of two chairs but they would not be likely to be very serious ones. The contestants would agree that it is not a matter in which one of them is right and the other wrong, as it is with the lengths. Each of them is entitled to his opinion. It is true that 'more comfortable' might be defined as what the majority find more comfortable, and some people might say that when they use the words they are not merely thinking of a private relationship, their own comfort. And since human beings are roughly of the same shape it will happen usually that there will be quite considerable agreement as to what chairs are or are not comfortable, though there is certainly also an element of habit and convention about it. The experts in comfort, the makers of arm-chairs and mattresses, make it their business to study intensively what human beings find comfortable and they may devise means of manufacturing objects to sit in or lie on which give greater and greater satisfaction in this respect. They certainly try to persuade the public in their advertisements that they are doing this. They are trying to discover facts about what opinions are, and at the same time trying to mould opinion. It will be a matter of fact that some chairs are generally found to be more comfortable than others, and for me to describe the reactions of people, including myself, is to state a fact. What my opinion is, is a fact, but the opinion itself remains an opinion.

Both the cases that we have considered so far are obvious and easy, and it may seem surprising that it has been thought worth while to discuss them at such length. Our reason for doing so is that the consideration of these cases at the two extremes provides a solid base from which to work for the discussion of trickier borderline cases.

When the comparison is one of length or weight or temperature or area or volume it is simply a question of taking the appropriate instruments and measuring. It may sometimes be necessary to clarify the issue by a more precise definition. If, for example, we are told that A is bigger than B and are checking this statement, we should want to know whether 'bigger than' refers to weight, length, surface area, volume or perhaps some combination of these. Which it was would clearly depend on the nature of A and B, and it is quite likely that the user of the phrase 'bigger than' would not have thought out very precisely what comparison he was making. But the point is that once the comparison is clearly defined, provided that it is something to which numerical values can be attached, a public test can be made and there is a right answer which is a matter of fact.

When, however, the individual who is making the comparison is talking about the effects which different objects or people have on him, he is giving the facts about his opinions, and there is no necessary reason why the same objects should have precisely the same effects on different people, though there may be many reasons why they will be likely to have similar effects.

ANALYSIS OF 'A MATTER OF OPINION'

It will be worth while at this stage analysing rather more closely what it is to be a matter of opinion. It is important to notice that 'opinion' in this context can be used in two rather different senses. I can ask someone which, in his opinion, is the nicer of two dishes; or I can ask my friend who is standing with me on the top of a hill which, in his opinion, is the farther away of two churches that we can see.

In the first case I am merely asking him which he prefers, what his own individual taste is; there can be no question of his answer being verified by me or anybody else, though it is possible that on tasting the dishes again he may change his mind or his preference. In the second case I am asking my friend to exercise his judgement of distance; the answer that he gives will be right or wrong and we can find out which by looking at the map; though if the distances are very nearly the same the map may not be sufficiently accurate to tell us and other methods and measurements may be necessary. For the moment we are going to concentrate our attention on the first sense of matters of opinion – matters of taste.

The example we took, which of two dishes was preferred, was obviously one where the use of the word 'taste' was entirely appropriate, though the word is also used – rather oddly – to express matters of preference where the other senses are concerned. We might say that it's a matter of feeling which of two chairs is more comfortable, that it's a matter of smell which of two odours is nicer; but these would probably be regarded as queer things to say. Or we might use the phrase 'a matter of preference'. On the whole this seems to be a situation in which the language which is ready to hand and is normally used is somewhat inadequate and inappropriate. Either we say it's a matter of opinion and run the risk of getting mixed up with the judgement sense of opinion – and it may well be that some quite serious muddles have resulted from these two notions masquerading as one; or we say it's a matter of taste and run the risk – probably a less serious one – of confusions arising from using the name of one of the senses for an expression of preference by any or all of them.

TASTE STATEMENTS OR STATEMENTS OF PREFERENCE

Taste statements or statements of preference which are frankly admitted to be subjective are perfectly straightforward and do not give rise to any particular problem as long as they are not disguised to appear objective but say exactly what is meant. When I say that I like beef, or that I prefer beef to mutton, there are no doubts or difficulties about the facts which are being described. I am talking about my reactions to the taste of different dishes, and assessing the comparative pleasure or pain derived from them. We all perform operations or make assessments of the same kind about all sorts of things – food, furniture, clothes, pictures, music, people. We know from the most direct and immediate kind of experience what it is to prefer, or to expect to prefer, one thing to another, and to make a statement or decide on a course of action based on this preference or this expectation. We are continually, consciously or unconsciously, forming and using a scale of preferences – though it may often be rather a vague one – and the examination or analysis of such scales of preferences, insofar as they apply to things which can be bought and sold, is an important part of the economist's task. The details of this process need not concern us now.

Although we are continually making such assessments we may often in fact find the task rather difficult. We're not really quite sure which we prefer, and we may leave the matter undecided until and unless we actually have to make a choice.

ACTS OF CHOICE

Implicit in a statement of preference is a statement of what one would choose if one had to, though it is certainly not the case that a statement of preference will always be followed by an act of choice. In real life the choices we have to make are bound to be particular ones in a certain context. At the lunch table, here and now, which will you have, this sweet or that? You have five shillings in your pocket and are hungry and thirsty; how will you spend your money? Would you prefer to play golf or go bathing this afternoon? But it would often not be legitimate to infer from these particular acts of choice a general preference. The lodger who in response to his landlady's inquiries nominates 'bubble and squeak' as his favourite among the dishes that the landlady has given him does not really mean to imply that always, on every occasion, he would rather have it than any of the others. If we are asked as a general question whether we prefer golf to bathing, or Shaw to Shakespeare, although some people might be able to give an unequivocal answer that always, under all circumstances they would prefer one to the other, or that generally speaking they derive more pleasure from one than from the other, many people would want to say that it all depends. Sometimes they prefer one, sometimes the other. It depends in the first case on the temperature, on how good the golf and bathing are, on whether one is feeling energetic or lazy. In the second case it depends on one's mood, on who is taking part if it is a question of seeing performances of the plays, on how hard one feels like thinking if it is just a question of reading them.

Again if we are asked which chair we find more comfortable the answer may well be that it all depends. More comfortable for what? For relaxing in front of the fire, or for sitting at one's desk and doing some work? However odd and outcast the chair, it may well be possible to find a purpose for which it would be more suitable to sit in, and therefore in a sense more comfortable, than its more frequently selected rivals.

It may often be rather irritating to be asked to express a preference of a very general kind when no particular act of choice is required, and such expression may seem artificial and unreal. It is worth noticing also that we don't normally make statements of preference between things which are very dissimilar. We would not in general ask someone 'Which do you prefer, rice pudding or Mr Jones?' though we may sometimes in fact have to take decisions which imply just that sort of choice. (Suppose for example that Mr Jones calls just as we're starting our rice pudding; he's an impatient person and he'll go if we keep him waiting; there are all sorts of reasons why we don't want him to go. But in this case, as in a vast number of cases where choices have to be made, there is likely to be a whole complex of motives of which the expression of a straight preference between rice pudding and Mr Jones would be an absurd simplification.)

It is at least doubtful whether a sincere taste-statement can be false. Can a man be wrong in thinking and saying that he prefers A to B? And can he be shown to be wrong? (The passage quoted in Exercise 5 [page 146] suggests that experts in modern consumer research think that he can be.) This is of course a different matter from a man changing his preference which is a thing that we all do frequently.

It is a commonplace of experience however that people do in fact often make false statements about their preferences, though sometimes for very worthy motives. Smith and Brown sit down to tea together and there are on the table two buns, one Bath, one Chelsea. Smith asks Brown which he prefers. Brown in fact would greatly prefer the Chelsea bun but, as he has reason to think that Smith would too, he unselfishly but untruthfully replies that he would like the Bath bun. This is in fact the bun for which Smith is longing, but for politeness sake he says that this will suit him very well as he has always preferred Chelsea buns. Each of them then eats the bun which he would rather not have. They may in fact both be compensated to some extent for the physical pleasure of which they are depriving themselves by a warm moral glow. People may also make false statements about their preferences if they think there are certain things they ought to like ('I adore Beethoven'), and may indulge only in private, tastes ('Pop' music, tripe and onions) which are thought to be not quite respectable.

MATTERS OF JUDGEMENT

We come now to consider the other sense of matters of opinion – matters of judgement. The example we took – estimating the comparative distance of two churches – was one where it was obvious that we were making a judgement about matters of fact, and that our judgement was open to confirmation or contradiction. This is a process with which we are all familiar. We judge distances, weights, ages, the number of sheep in a field, whether Blenkinsop is telling the truth, what really happened at a certain place at a certain time, who's going to win the 2.30, whether it's going to rain this afternoon. Some of these judgements are of present situations, some of what happened in the past; some are predictions about what is going to happen in the future. On the whole they are inferences from evidence which may be more or less complete; they may be carefully thought out judgements made by an intelligent person based on much relevant experience, or they may be merely wild guesses. What they all have in common however is that they are judgements about matters of fact, that they are true or false, though in some particular cases, for example about events in the past, we may never know which. In general there are no great difficulties or problems about the analysis of judgements of this kind, at the level at which we are discussing matters. It is worth noticing however that judgements of matters of fact include judgements about what people's preferences are or are going to be. Preferring is a matter of taste, what people do in fact prefer or choose – for example how they cast their votes in an election – is a matter of fact.

VALUE JUDGEMENTS

Taste statements and fact judgements lie at extreme ends of the scale. We come now to consider a whole class of expressions of opinion which lie between the two, or about which a vital and interesting thing to be decided is to which of the two they belong. Such statements may be broadly classed as value judgements. We make a value judgement whenever we give a mark or a rating to one thing in comparison with another, whenever we say that A is better than B using 'better' in its broadest, loosest sense. When a schoolmaster gives 35 marks out of 50 to one essay and 29 to another he is making what would ordinarily be called a value judgement. The interesting question that arises however from our discussion in this chapter so far, is whether what he is doing is more closely akin to what one is doing when one says that this stick is longer than that, or to what is being done when one says that this chair is more comfortable than that. Is it a judgement about a matter of fact (in which case it is perfectly possible for it to be an incorrect one) or is it just the expression of a personal preference? Is the judgement objective or subjective?

It is probable that few people would wish to hold either extreme position about this kind of judgement, this act of assessment. Can it really be maintained that the comparative merit to be attached to the essays of, say, a class of 20 is a matter of fact to which there is a precise correct answer, laid up as it were in heaven, if only we can find it? It is worth noticing here that there are two difficulties involved – first the *order* of merit of the different essays and secondly by *how much* one is better than the other. Would it be possible to maintain not only that A's is better than B's and B's better than C's but also that the difference between A's and B's is, say, exactly 2·5 times the difference between B's and C's? (This two-fold difficulty is of course implicit in all scales of preferences or evaluations. To place them simply in an order of merit is to use an *Ordinal* scale; to maintain that it is possible to evaluate the relative amounts by which some are to be preferred to others is to believe in the possibility of a *Cardinal* scale.)

But on the other hand if one discards this view as repugnant to common sense, is one therefore to say that it is simply a matter of taste? That the schoolmaster is arranging the essays in the order which he personally finds pleasing just as he might, if asked, arrange in the order which he finds pleasing a number of dishes? In this case is one bound to say (as one would certainly say as far as the dishes were concerned) that there is no question of his being right or wrong, that any one person's opinion is as good as any other's, or rather that there is no sense in which one can talk about anyone's opinion being 'good'?

Our natural reaction is to say that the truth lies somewhere in between these two extremes. It might also be a natural reaction to object to the last sentences of the preceding paragraph, to say that in a matter of this kind one person's opinion is *not* as good as any other person's, that there is in fact such a thing as an expert opinion.

We must now investigate more closely how, if at all, it is possible to take up a position between the view that marking an essay is a judgement of matters of fact and the view that it is simply an expression of personal preference: we must also examine the concept of expert opinion in this context.

Before we return to the schoolmaster and his essays it will be useful to bring out a few points by considering some other value judgements. Suppose we say 'A is better at chess than B'. Chess is a game and the object is to win. The test therefore for deciding whether A is better than B is the factual, objective one of A playing chess against B – preferably several times – and seeing who wins. If A wins on each occasion easily (i.e. quickly) we should feel justified in saying that the statement is true and that it is a matter of fact. Suppose however that someone who has watched all these games denies this proposition and asserts that in spite of all his defeats B is *really* a better chess player. What should we say to him? It would clearly be natural and fair to ask him what he means by B being better. Perhaps he might say that B is potentially a better player. If A is middle-aged and B a small boy it might be felt that A has won his victories because of his greater experience, but that B has displayed in his style of play a superior grasp of the essential principles which may well make him a very strong player one day. Any sensible discussion about the matter would then be focused on the question whether by A being 'better than' B at chess we are going to mean A having a recent record of victories over B or whether we are going to use the phrase to refer to the probability of B being able to defeat A consistently at some unspecified date in the future. In fact, without defining the matter very accurately, we may well use the phrase to mean some rather vague combination of both; partly a matter of fact, who has won more games of chess; and partly a matter of prediction, who is likely to win more games of chess in the future. Most people in making the judgement as to who is the better chess player are likely to attach considerably more weight to the first of these considerations. It is possible that someone who is making a judgement about two chess players might also consider their styles. B might be a lively, attacking, enterprising player while A's style is dull, stodgy, safe. Even though A won more often it might still be maintained by some people that B was the 'better' player. It would be reasonable in such a case to point out that the criterion for being a good chess player must surely be to win or to be likely to win games of chess and that, unless it is claimed that this dashing style may make success in the future more likely, the word 'better' is being used in an odd and irrational sense.

Chess is one of the games in which it is least likely that a consideration of style will form part of the criteria of merit. It is much more likely to happen with a game like cricket when we are considering the rival merits of two batsmen. It would be reasonable to suppose that the criterion for being a 'good' batsman is to score runs or at least to stay in, and that the better batsman will be the one who scores more runs against the same, or approximately equally 'good', bowling; we might also take into consideration the rate at which those runs are scored.

It is common practice however to include also in one's consideration the 'style' or the method in which the runs are made. A good style for a batsman should presumably mean those methods of batting which make it more likely or are thought to make it more likely that he will remain at the wicket and score runs. But there may also enter into it the question of taste; I call A a better batsman because I find his style more pleasing, attractive. It may be argued that if this more attractive style is not actually or potentially the source of more runs I am *wrong* in so calling him. It is nevertheless the case that different people will use the phrase 'good batsman' in slightly different ways, and it is important to notice that what is being done is to some extent reporting on matters of fact, to some extent making a prediction about the future and to some extent expressing a taste preference. 'Better' is inevitably a very vague and loose word in this sort of context and it is always an aid to clear thinking (though sometimes it may be unnecessarily long-winded) if one specifies in what respect better ('more pleasing to watch, though he doesn't make so many runs') instead of using vague terms of commendation.

One more example before we return to our schoolmaster and his essays. Suppose we want to decide whether A or B is the better runner. A can beat B comfortably and consistently over short distances, say less than half a mile; and B can beat A equally comfortably and consistently over any distance more than a mile. Which is the better runner? Obviously the criterion for being a 'good' runner is to run fast. Questions of style may come into it, but again, as with the batsman at cricket, the essentials of a good style at running will be based on principles of efficiency, principles which, if observed, will help one to run more rapidly. The facts in our example are that A is better than B over some distances, B is better than A over others (presumably one could find some intermediate distance over which the result of a race between them would be a dead-heat). If asked to say which is the better, one is being asked to make a comparative assessment of the amount by which A is better than B in one respect and the amount by which B is better than A in another. This is obviously a very difficult thing to do. One could work out a system of marking based on comparative times at different distances and thus define what it is to be a better runner, but any such system would inevitably have an element of arbitrariness about it, and in the last resort it is a matter of opinion, of taste. There is certainly no correct answer. It may well be thought (and I hope that readers are thinking this) that it is a silly question. Why can't we just state what the facts are, who beats whom at what distances? Why do we have to have a comprehensive, overall evaluation?

(An answer might very likely be that there is a cup to be awarded to the 'best' runner, so that a decision or choice has to be made.)

This is a simple version of a process which happens a great deal, though it is a process which may to some extent be wrapped up and disguised. It is not merely the difficulty of the cardinal scale of values to which we referred earlier – the difficulty of comparing the amount by which we prefer A to B to the amount by which we prefer B to C, when A, B and C are of the same kind (e.g. dishes to eat) and the criteria for our preference are of the same sort (tasting nice). It is the difficulty of comparing the amount by which A is superior to B in one respect to the amount by which X is superior to Y in another. (Do you like strawberries better than blackberries by as much as you prefer Ermyntrude to Clarissa?) Obviously if one *has* to give an answer to this question – if one's life depends on it – one will give it, and in fact people are continually making value judgements of this kind. The answer that one gives is not verifiable or falsifiable and certainly it may sometimes be felt that one can answer with conviction and confidence.

(Suppose, for example, that one is passionately fond of strawberries, heartily dislikes blackberries and has only just haltingly, waveringly and without much assurance come to the point of feeling a preference for Ermyntrude rather than Clarissa.)

On the whole most people are likely to feel that the question is a silly one; they might rather resent being forced to give an answer to it, and might feel that any answer they gave would just be the result of a mental toss-up. (How does one set about answering a question like that? Through what mental process is one supposed to go?) And it might well be felt also that to answer a question like that could not conceivably serve any useful purpose.

Answers to similar questions however are implicit in a great many of the evaluations which we do in fact make.

Our diversion from the schoolmaster and his essays was designed to make, by considering simpler cases, three main points:

1. The criteria for being 'better' depend on the purposes of what are being considered. If people are being compared in some particular capacity, for example as chess-players or batsmen, we mean by this the purposes which they have in mind, to win games of chess or to make runs. If physical objects are being compared, for example if we ask which is the 'better' of two houses, we mean the purposes for which

they are to be used, to house two people in a cold climate or ten people in a warm one, or whatever it may be.

2. Some of the criteria may be matters of fact in the present, some may be concerned with predictions about what is going to happen in the future, and some may be matters of taste. It is unlikely to be the case that all those who make value judgements about the same things will use precisely the same criteria, though they will generally be at least similar.

3. As we saw in the example of the runners some value judgements will entail a process of comparing the importance or the value of differences between things in one respect, which may itself be a matter of fact or a matter of taste, with differences between the same or other things in another respect. P is a better batsman than Q, but Q is a better bowler. Which is the better cricketer? X is better than Y at French and History, but Y is better at Latin and Mathematics. Which is the cleverer? In some cases in a particular context an act of choice may be necessary: shall I select P or Q for my team tomorrow? But this depends on other circumstances (e.g. the comparative batting and bowling strength of the rest of the team), and need not imply a generalized value judgement. The number of respects in which a comparison is being made obviously need not be limited to two or three or four.

The process we have been describing, the portmanteau value judgement to cover many different comparisons which may themselves be somewhat suspect, is always difficult and might often be reasonably described as impossible or unreal.

.We return now to the schoolmaster and his essays. What he is doing is to make comparative value judgements which purport to be precise. He is guided to some extent in making these judgements by matters of fact, whether for example the spelling conforms to the precise rules which exist, whether the punctuation and grammar are correct, though for these the rules are considerably less precise. He is also assessing, perhaps, the extent to which the essays have included certain basic bits of information, certain matters of fact which were parts of what he, the setter of the essay, wanted, the extent to which the writer shows himself well informed about those matters of which his knowledge is being tested. He is also probably assessing the extent to which the writer has succeeded in communicating his ideas clearly, interestingly and entertainingly, and in doing this the schoolmaster will be thinking not only whether he himself is interested and entertained, but also whether others of similar intelligence and education would be likely to be so too. He will be assessing the extent to which the writer has succeeded in achieving the purposes which were set before him.

Some of these assessments are matters of fact, some are matters of taste (whether the reader finds it interesting), some are judgements or predictions about the tastes of other people. What then has to be done is to combine these assessments of different things into an overall value judgement to which a precise numerical value will be attached. The comparative heinousness of a mistake in spelling, an error in punctuation, getting a fact wrong, and being dull, has to to be decided. Such comparison is clearly a matter of opinion or taste to which, unlike some of the other assessments that are being made, the notion of expert opinion (to which we shall return later) is hardly applicable. (It is perhaps worth noticing that the schoolmaster may often use marks not simply to measure the gravity of an offence, but as an incentive or deterrent. Brown really must pay more attention to his spelling and to writing legibly, and to encourage him to do so a disproportionately large number of marks may be taken off for failures in these respects.)

It might be said that this operation, this comparison of the size of value differences of different kinds ending up with a result that seems by implication to claim to be precise, is so absurd, is so obviously (especially to anyone who has tried to do it) not precise, that one wonders why it is done.

It is of course the result of a tendency, which seems to become more marked as the world becomes more competitive, to want to put things and people in an order of merit. It is partly because it has come to be thought that since with the advance of science man has increasingly succeeded in measuring things, everything (intelligence, literary skill, etc.) is measurable, and there has grown up the very dangerous tendency to try to be precise or to claim to be precise when no precision is possible, and to suppose, when there is a failure to achieve precision, that this is due to some inadequacy in ourselves or in our tools or methods of measurement, instead of being due, as is very often the case, to the nature of what is being considered.

Only by drawing up a clear-cut precise scale of values or marks for different points could it be said that one essay was worth 35 marks and another 29, but the drawing up of this scale of values would be to introduce an artificial precision concerning what is bound in the last analysis to be a matter of opinion or taste.

Nevertheless, although the precision implicit in the numerical evaluation of essays may be generally speaking unjustified and artificial, it is certainly and obviously not the case that the operation of marking essays is without value. As we have pointed out the writer is trying to achieve certain purposes (for example to be intelligible and interesting) and the schoolmaster is assessing the extent to which these purposes have been achieved as far as his reactions are concerned and are likely to be achieved with regard to the reactions of other people. Experiments are often made to determine the extent to which different examiners agree about the comparative merits of essays and, as might be expected, although agreement on the whole is not very close, it is usually close enough to provide some justification for the operation of marking. In other words there is likely to be a consensus of opinion that certain essays are more intelligible and interesting than others even though it is not possible to measure by how much. If however the assessment of some few examiners is markedly different from that of the majority, this may well be thought to show how little the few know about it, that they are not experts; and it might be maintained that the more 'expert' the opinion the greater the measure of agreement is likely to be.

The time has come to examine rather more closely the concept of 'expert opinion', to see what part, if any, it has to play in affairs which are matters of taste.

EXPERT OPINION

Let us take a simple case first, the comparative 'comfortableness' of a number of chairs; a case where the comparison would be generally agreed to be subjective and not a matter of fact. Is there any sense in which it would be reasonable to talk about expert opinion in this context?

What the expert can do is to study the human frame and the feeling-reactions of himself and other people to chairs of various shapes and designs, and to make deductions and generalizations about what people do find comfortable and are likely to find comfortable and why. The advice of such an expert will be useful to the manufacturers of the chairs and also to individuals who are selecting chairs. 'This chair here, for example, you may not find very comfortable when you first sit in it, but my experience and that of other people has been that if you try it for a bit and get used to it you will eventually find it more comfortable than anything you have ever sat in; you will get a higher quality of comfort-pleasure than you have ever received.'

What the expert does is to advise people how their tastes may be best satisfied, how the purpose of giving or getting comfort-pleasure is most likely to be achieved. And he becomes an expert by studying the subject matter.

Similarly an expert in food may advise people what they are likely to enjoy tasting, and make recommendations whereby they may increase the pleasure of eating. Just as, since people are constructed in roughly the same way, there are certain general principles derived from experience as to what they are likely to find most comfortable, so since people's palates and taste buds are similarly constructed there are certain general principles as to what they are most likely to enjoy eating. But these general principles are clearly not precise, there will be many exceptions, they will vary from one community to another, and there will certainly be elements of habit and convention in the formation of these principles.

Notice that the expert may make statements about what people are likely to find comfortable and what they are likely to find nice and these statements may be verified or falsified by events (and the verification of his statements will also serve to some extent as a verification of his expert status). It would however be misleading if he were to make statements about what *is* comfortable, what *is* nice; if his statements instead of appearing to be predictions or recommendations, were to be interpreted as telling people what they *ought* to find comfortable to sit in or nice to eat.

In fact this is not at all likely to happen with comfort, and not very likely to happen with food. It is rather more likely however to happen with wine. The expert in this case becomes the 'connoisseur'. He will be knowledgeable and an expert not only in the sense that he is likely to be able to tell the source and perhaps even the date of a wine by tasting it but also that what he says about which wines are good will be accepted as authoritative and right. When he says that one wine is 'better' than another, however, it may sometimes be thought that he is doing something rather more than, and different from, making a prediction about which wine people in general will prefer. But obviously wines are for drinking and it can hardly make sense to use any criterion for judging the comparative merits of wines other than the extent to which people enjoy drinking them, though one might certainly include under 'enjoyment' here, not only the experience at the time but also the after-effects, pleasant or otherwise, any curative or toxic properties that the wine might have. The connoisseur however might make the claim that even though the majority of people would prefer A to B, nevertheless B is better than A. What could be meant by such a claim and can it be substantiated?

Such a claim could clearly only be based on the pleasure that *someone* derives from drinking it. He might say that the pleasure that the expert derives from B is of a higher quality than that derived from A, and that if other people had the opportunities and would take the trouble to train their palates they too would appreciate this. He is making the recommendation that potentially the pleasure derivable from B is to be preferred or would in general be preferred to that derived from A. This recommendation or prediction is in principle verifiable and would seem to provide a reasonable basis for the expert to say that B is better than A.

Let us see now how the concept of expert opinion applies to the schoolboy's essays or rather to the field of literature in general.

EXPERT OPINION AND LITERATURE

The purposes of literature are considerably less clear-cut and more various than the purposes of the chair, the food or the wine. They may be to inform, to explain, to communicate ideas, to stimulate new ways of looking at things, to amuse, to entertain, to persuade, to rouse emotions, to communicate deep emotional experiences or to provide them. It has been said that 'the study of it [the literary critic's literature] is, or should be, an intimate study of the complexities, potentialities and essential conditions of human nature.' (F. R. LEAVIS, *The Common Pursuit*, p. 184.) The purposes of the schoolboy's essay must certainly be included among the general purposes of literature, it should be an exercise in achieving one or more of these purposes, and its 'value' should clearly depend on the extent to which it does these things or is thought to be likely to do these things. All these purposes, it should be noticed, are expressed in terms of the effects which the literature has on those who read it; literature is for reading as wine is for drinking. But though drinking is for pleasure, reading need not be.

Clearly the 'expert' about literature – the literary critic, the schoolmaster, the university don – in expressing an opinion about the merits of a certain work, will be partly making an assessment about matters of fact – whether what is written is true, accurate, properly spelt and punctuated and grammatically expressed (though it is only in certain departments of literature that these things will necessarily be counted as merits); partly assessing the extent to which the work does to him what it is intended to do – entertain, delight, interest, inform, instruct, emotionally move or generally improve – and partly making a prediction about the extent to which it is likely to do these things to other people, perhaps especially in some cases a particular class of other people, those who are also 'experts' in the relevant field.

Literary critics would be the first to express relief at the fact that on the whole they are not expected when writing their criticisms or opinions to attach a precise mark to various works as the schoolmaster is often impelled to do to his essay, though they may sometimes attach 'ratings', they may sometimes produce a list of the ten 'best' books of the year or of the century, and they will almost certainly attach to the books they review adjectives, usually rather vague ones of approval or disapproval. To what extent then, if any, can it be said that literary merit is a matter of fact, objective, and to what extent a matter of taste, subjective?

There is no doubt that the experts, the literary critics, do often write as though literary merit was something objective as though there was a sense in which it could be said that some books were 'better' than others and that anybody who thought otherwise was just wrong. They would be likely to maintain stoutly that majority opinion is not what determines whether a book is 'good' or not, and it is often implied that, though its merit is obviously much more likely to be discovered by expert opinion, there is a sense in which that merit would still be 'there' whether the experts discovered it or not.

Those who disagree with the concept of literary merit as being something objective, valid for all men, would maintain that all that the critic can usefully and justifiably do by way of assessment is to report on the effect that the work has on him, perhaps to suggest reasons why this effect is as it is, and explicitly or implicitly to make a prediction about the effect it is likely to have on other people. Any prediction of this kind that he makes about opinions would itself be objective and capable in principle of verification or falsification. But again the opinion itself remains an opinion. It is sometimes claimed that literary effects are capable of being exceedingly important; the study of literature may be regarded 'not only as a discipline in itself, but as a social and moral force, at once a prophylactic and a remedy for the corruption and degradation inherent in our materialistic society' (J. B. Bamborough, *Spectator*, 25 October 1963, describing a conviction attributed to F. R. Leavis). But the importance of the effect makes no difference to the argument that it will vary from person to person.

In admitting the fact that the experts hold strong views about their scales of preferences and sometimes, but by no means always, agree among themselves on a preference that is contrary to majority preference, the subjectivists might introduce the idea of a higher quality of pleasure and a progression, as a result of expert knowledge and experience, from a lower quality to a higher. It is a matter of fact for example that the writings of Jane Austen will generally be described as 'better than' those of, say, Edgar Wallace, in spite of the probability that they have been read and enjoyed by many fewer people. Although the phrase 'better than' in such a context is hopelessly vague, it is used. Let us try to consider what might be meant by it.

An objectivist might support such a statement by saying that the works of Jane Austen possess greater literary merit and that anyone who thinks otherwise is lacking in literary appreciation and is just wrong. A subjectivist might reply that this is a misleading way of describing the facts. One can say that some people prefer Jane Austen, others Edgar Wallace, and that though there can be no question of either group being right or wrong, it is nevertheless a fact that those who study the matter closely and do a lot of reading find that the pleasure or general benefit they get from Jane Austen seems to them to be of a higher quality; many cases are found of people progressing, as they would describe it, from Wallace to Austen, but not many cases of people making a similar change of preference from Austen to Wallace. (It is possible of course that this description as 'progression' may itself be influenced by what would be a widely held view that one 'ought' to prefer Austen to Wallace.)

Those who have made such a progression feel entitled therefore to recommend that others should do likewise. They point to the superior intellectual pleasures that may be derived from the study of 'good' literature in the same sort of way as the expert on food and drink may draw attention to the superior tasting-pleasures that may be derived from the cultivation of the palate and the study of 'good' cooking. The subjectivist might make the further point that he would not want to express an overall prefer-ence for one author over another. It all depends – on one's mood, on whether one wants to be relaxed or stimulated and so on. And he would say that it is sensible to distinguish between the selection that he makes at a particular moment, and the opinion that he expresses about the comparative satisfaction, instruction, benefit, that might be derived from reading them under the most suitable conditions.

'But yet', the objectivists might reply, 'everyone knows that some books *are* better than others; this alternative way of describing it can't disguise the fact that either a book has literary merit or not. And once this is admitted to be a matter of opinion, there are no standards, everything is shifting and chaos reigns.' Objectivists also tend to feel that the subjectivist view degrades the importance of literature and the intellectual and aesthetic delights that can be derived from it.

To the first objection the subjectivist would reply that there are certainly no absolute standards in the matter, and that 'literary merit' as it seems to be thought about by his opponent is a myth; he is thinking about it in the wrong way and the objection begs the question. He would go on to say that the absence of absolute standards, valid for all men, and the emphasis on opinion or taste need in no way lessen the pleasures, perhaps the improvement, to be derived from literature, or alter the fact that such experiences are usually regarded by those who have had them as preferable to the pleasures of the table.

This discussion of literary merit is at a deliberately inexpert level. The experts, and perhaps even more the knowledgeable amateurs, tend to be emotionally involved and they may well feel that what has been said here shows insufficient knowledge. I would suggest that the principles of what is happening and the subjectivity of value judgements do not depend at all on details of what these judgements are or how they are arrived at.

The arguments about the subjectivist view of value judgements of beauty tend to be similar to those we have been considering in discussing literary merit. Let us take a look at them.

VALUE JUDGEMENTS OF BEAUTY

Next to value judgements about ethics those about beauty are the trickiest and most difficult to discuss. In the past certainly, though this is probably less true today, views about them have often been held with passion and in any discussion it is advisable to tread warily and to treat delicately notions which are likely to be emotionally cherished as well as being entertained with strong intellectual conviction.

An enormous amount has been written about the theory of beauty or the philosophy of beauty, and in a brief discussion there is the inevitable risk that we lay ourselves open to the charge of over-simplification. In particular we shall try to show how the general arguments we have been developing about value judgements apply to value judgements of beauty, and we shall consider especially the contrast between the objective and the subjective view of the matter. It is hardly necessary to say that any detailed consideration of the qualities which make a thing beautiful would be irrelevant.

There is not much doubt that the view that has been most strongly held by philosophers in the past, from Plato onwards, has been the objective one – that is that beauty in a sense is something that is *there*, that whether an object is beautiful or not is a matter of fact and not a matter of opinion or taste, and that value judgements about beauty are true or false, right or wrong.

Plato believed that there were two orders of reality, the world of everyday experience, of becoming and change, which was not truly real, and the world of ultimate, unchangeable reality, the world of 'Forms'. These forms were such entities as Absolute Beauty, or Goodness, or Squareness or Justice, and a particular object in the world of appearances was beautiful in so far as it participated in the Form of Absolute Beauty or in so far as that Form was manifested in the object. Whether a thing was beautiful or not was therefore a matter of fact. The following quotations from Plato and others are examples of the generally held view of the objectivity of beauty.

Your lovers of sights and sounds delight in beautiful tones and colours and shapes and in all the works of art into which these enter; but they have not the power of thought to behold and to take delight in the nature of Beauty itself.

That power to approach Beauty and behold it as it is in itself is rare indeed. PLATO, *The Republic*, trans. by F. Cornford, p. 179.

What may we suppose to be the felicity of the man who sees absolute beauty in its essence, pure and unalloyed, who . . . is able to apprehend divine beauty where it exists apart and alone? PLATO, *The Symposium*, trans. by W. Hamilton, p. 95.

Beauty consists in a certain size and arrangement of parts. ARISTOTLE, *Poetics*.

. . . the statement, not I think contradicted by the unsophisticated mind, that judgements of taste claim to be valid for all men, while judgements on what is agreeable are purely subjective. E. F. CARRITT, *The Theory of Beauty*, p. 6. (In the context he is using the phrase 'judgements of taste' to refer to judgements about what things are beautiful.)

. . . it (beauty) does claim that its recognition is universally valued for humanity, that is to say is in a sense 'true'. Ibid., p. 7.

... those who have practised more arts than one, in a greater degree even than those who have appreciated many, are aware that in every picture, in every art, and wherever it is found in nature, in a dance, in the sea, in tragedy, in a sunset, and in music, beauty is unequivocally beauty. Ibid., p. 12.

Kant holds truly that in an aesthetic experience we do believe ourselves to be in some sense right; that to it, unlike our gustatory experiences, we give objective value. Ibid., p. 72.

It has been more commonly supposed that the beautiful may be *defined* as that which produces certain effects upon our feelings; and the conclusion which follows from this – namely, that judgements of taste are merely *subjective* – that precisely the same thing may, according to circumstances, be *both* beautiful *and* not beautiful – has very frequently been drawn. The conclusions of this chapter suggest a definition of beauty which may partially explain and entirely remove the difficulties which have led to this error. It appears probable that the beautiful should be *defined* as that of which the admiring contemplation is good in itself. That is to say: To assert that a thing is beautiful is to assert that the cognition of it is an essential element in one of the intrinsically valuable wholes we have been discussing; so that the question whether it is truly beautiful or not, depends upon the *objective* question whether the whole in question is or is not truly good, and does not depend upon the question whether it would or would not excite particular feelings in particular persons. G. E. MOORE, *Principia Ethica*, p. 201.

Passages expressing the contrary opinion are, certainly until recently, less frequently to be found in the writings of philosophers. David Hume, the eighteenth-century Scottish philosopher, summed the matter up succinctly thus:

Handsome and beautiful, on most occasions, is not an absolute but a relative quality and pleases us by nothing but its tendency to produce an end that is agreeable. *A Treatise of Human Nature* III. iii. I.

There is no doubt that a strong reason in the past for maintaining the objectivity of beauty has been the feeling that if it were subjective its worth and importance would be diminished. That the niceness of food is a matter of taste, subjective, has probably been almost always generally agreed by mankind, but the beauty of art or of nature arouses in us feelings which seem to be of so much more elevated and sublime a character that to say that this too is a matter of taste or subjective has seemed to many people to be degrading the pleasures of aesthetic appreciation down to the level of the pleasures of the table.

This feeling about the intrinsic worth or importance of beauty, that it is something which is not only valid for all men, absolute, but also that it should be pursued for its own sake, is well illustrated by the following passage from G. E. Moore:

Let us imagine one world exceedingly beautiful. Imagine it as beautiful as you can; put into it whatever on this earth you most admire – mountains, rivers, the sea; trees, and sunsets, stars and moon. Imagine these all combined in the most exquisite proportions, so that no one thing jars against another, but each contributes to increase the beauty of the whole. And then imagine the ugliest world you can possibly conceive. Imagine it simply one heap of filth, containing everything that is most disgusting to us, for whatever reason, and the whole, as far as may be, without one redeeming feature. ... The only thing we are not entitled to imagine is that any human being ever has or ever, by any possibility, *can*, live in either, can ever see and enjoy the beauty of the one or hate the foulness of the other. Well, even so, supposing them quite apart from any possible contemplation by human beings; still, is it irrational to hold that it is better that the beautiful world should exist, than the one which is ugly ? *Principia Ethica*, Chapter 3.

This passage was written in criticism of Sidgwick, who had said:

No one would consider it rational to aim at the production of beauty in external nature, apart from any possible contemplation of it by human beings.

It is interesting that this same thought is echoed by a later writer:

No one now imagines that a work of art lying on an uninhabited island has absolute value. CLIVE BELL, *Civilization*, p. 61.

Most people today would, I think, agree with Sidgwick and Bell rather than Moore. 'Better in what way and for what purpose ?' one would want to ask him. For the notion of good-in-itself would seem on analysis to be somewhat empty and meaningless. In this particular case it seems to us that it is not 'better-in-itself' but rather, 'preferable-to-imagine' that Moore must mean, and can only sensibly mean, though no doubt he would have denied this himself. Notice that if we shift the emphasis to individuals taking pleasure from looking at various objects rather than the intrinsic merits that the objects are supposed to have, not only do we find ourselves talking in terms that are readily intelligible about matters that are derived from experience, but a whole set of philosophical problems connected with the notion of 'good-in-itself' fade away.

In many spheres the idea of intrinsic value is less readily accepted now than it was. Just as people are more likely to regard value in economics as dependent and relative so they are less likely to believe that absolute, objective beauty is a sensible or possible concept. This shift in opinion is certainly caused in part by the increasing realization that different people at different times and places have derived pleasurable aesthetic experience in very various ways. The more this happens the harder it is to maintain the position that value judgements of beauty are 'valid for all men', that 'in an aesthetic experience we are in some sense right'.

It is perhaps also true that experts today are more likely than they have sometimes been in the past to frame their opinions in the form of recommendation and advice rather than in the form of a dogmatic statement of value. They are more likely to suggest that a rewarding aesthetic experience may be the result of a detailed study of a work of art, more likely to say 'If you don't enjoy that I am sorry for you' than 'If you don't think that's beautiful, you're wrong.'

Again, as a matter of experience, it can be discovered that an aesthetic experience can be no less pleasurable, elevated, sublime, even though it is seen not to be valid for all men, that its value is not diminished, because different people get aesthetic satisfaction in different ways, and standards are not claimed to be absolute.

We have drawn attention to the fact that value judgements of beauty today are perhaps less generally agreed than they have sometimes been in the past, that they are less 'valid for all men', and we have suggested this as a contributory reason for the weakening of the notion of the objectivity of beauty. It is important however to notice again that what is being referred to is not merely a *universal* opinion (still less a *majority* one) but a *necessary* one. If a judgement about a chair being comfortable was agreed by everyone who had ever sat in it (and as a matter of interest one is likely to find greater agreement about chairs being comfortable than about pictures being beautiful), no one, I think, would want to claim that it was objective, nor would it be likely that the

phrase 'valid for all men' would be applied to it in the same
sense as it has been applied to judgements about beauty. It
would still be felt that someone might come along and find
it uncomfortable, and if he did we would not want to say
that he was wrong. The phrase 'valid for all men' has
normally been used not to describe an empirical fact but to
imply a *necessary* validity and we would certainly not feel
this about the chair being comfortable.

In other words a universal consensus of opinion about
comfort does not make people feel that such judgements are
objective, and the basic reason of course is that it is recognized that what is being talked about is a *relationship*
between an object and a person, or the senses of that
person. And it seems contrary to common sense (and in
general to experience) to suppose that the effects of this
relationship *must* necessarily be the same or that there is any
sense of the word in which they 'ought' always to be the
same. To talk about the comfort of chairs is to describe a
private experience. To make an objective statement
('Every chair in this room is occupied') is to describe a
public fact.

SUMMARY

It has been suggested in this chapter that there is no reason
why the arguments which apply to the pleasures of the
senses of the less elevated kind (comfort-pleasure, food-
tasting pleasure) should not similarly apply in principle to
the pleasures of a more elevated kind which we call
aesthetic. And we have suggested also that similar arguments apply to the intellectual experiences, pleasurable and
otherwise, which are derived from literature.

With regard to comfort and food, tastes differ; there are

no objective absolute standards but certain very useful empirical principles which 'experts' may to some extent discover and develop. These are the pleasures which come through the senses of touch and of taste. We have suggested that there seems no reason to suppose that the pleasures which come through the senses of smell or hearing or sight are different in kind. Different people take pleasure from looking at, smelling or listening to different things; there are no objective standards but certain general principles and in some respects considerable agreement. Again, different people are affected in different ways by the study of literature. The effects which certain writings and paintings and music have on some people may be very important, very sublime, but it still remains the case that there are no objective absolute standards, merely a large number of individual relationships between a person and what he reads, sees or hears. We might also add, though this would be too large a question to explore in detail here, that different people find different things funny; once more there are no objective standards but certain rather elusive general principles. Different people again fall in love with different members of the opposite sex: there are no objective standards here, no rules that are 'valid' for all men – and how fortunate for the future of the race that this is so.[1] And if there is talk of a lack of objectivity degrading the value of what is being experienced one might protest that there is surely no more elevated emotion than that of falling in love.

As a postscript to this chapter it is interesting to speculate

1. 'Sex attraction is so purely a question of the taste of the individual that the wise man never argues about it.' P. G. WODEHOUSE, *The Man with Two Left Feet and Other Stories*, p. 48.

on the extent to which language has influenced, or been influenced by, the way in which we think about the objectivity
or otherwise of certain qualities. In English, the adjective
'beautiful' is derived from the noun 'beauty'; whereas the
noun 'niceness' is derived from the adjective 'nice'.
Therefore, it might be suggested, we tend to think of beauty
as an objective entity of which various things may be more or
less 'full', but since the adjective 'nice' came before the
noun we are less likely to objectify the quality. It might also
be suggested that the language reflects the notion of those
who formed it. It would be relevant to consider too the
further point that the English noun is derived from the
French adjective *beau* and that yet another noun 'beautiful-
ness' (used by CLIVE BELL, *Civilization*, p. 63) has been
derived from the adjective 'beautiful'.

Exercises

1. 'If A is better than B, and B is better than C, then A is
better than C.' Comment.

2. Do you make a distinction between poems you like
and poems you think good? If so, what are your criteria?

3. The following is an extract from a letter to *The Times*
from Sir Hugh Casson (20 September 1963).

I am delighted to know that no final decision on the colour
[of a new London bus] has been made and hope it will not be
determined by finance alone. To be guided in these matters
by money values means really to be guided by no values at all.

   Analyse carefully the last sentence. Do you agree with it?

4. Consider and discuss the criteria you would use if you
had to judge the following contests. To what extent would
they be matters of fact, and to what extent matters of taste?

Would you be likely to have to compare the amount by which A was better than B in one respect with the amount by which B was better than A in another?

i. A Drill Competition

ii. A Flower Show

iii. A Music Competition

iv. A Beauty Contest

5. An article in the *Observer* about advertising (Paul Ferris, 22 September 1963) tells of a new way of testing consumer reactions by an eye-camera which measures changes in the pupil of the eye when it looks at things.

'The consumer is not an accurate reporter of his desires', said a man at Interpublic [An American advertising agency]. 'Instead of asking him if he likes a proposed advertisement or container, and letting loose his inhibitions and rationalizations, the investigator shows him the object and observes what happens to his pupils. His eye movements can be plotted at the same time, and a diagram prepared showing how he reacted to different parts of the ad. First, he doesn't know how he's supposed to respond. Second he can't do anything about it. That's the beauty of this.'

Do you think that you are an accurate reporter of your desires? Discuss whether this method is likely to lead to a truer assessment of individual evaluations.

6. 'Sure in the independence, confident of the future of Britain, the *Daily Express* is rooted in the hearts of the people.

It is Britain's greatest newspaper.'

Daily Express, 31 December 1960.

Discuss the possible criteria for this claim.

7. 'The comfortable is everything that is or will be so called by those who have employed or shall employ the name.'

(*a*) Do you agree?

(*b*) For 'comfortable' substitute 'sublime'. (It then becomes a quotation from the Italian philosopher, Benedetto Croce.) Do you agree now?

8. Discuss whether the person who described criticism as 'a hazel-switch for the discovery of buried treasure, not a birch twig for the castigation of offenders' took a subjective or objective view of the matter.

9. '. . . is too good a critic to judge a production from the surface only; instead he makes it his business to look at the play in depth and assess it in terms of *real* values.'
(From an advertisement for the *Sunday Telegraph* in the *Listener*, 17 October 1963.)
Analyse the likely meaning of '*real* values' in this context.

10. In a review in the *New Statesman* (25 October 1963) Professor D. W. Harding writes that both the authors whose books he is reviewing:

would presumably agree in thinking that literature and science each achieve its own form of precision in the use of language: science an analytic precision in which a statement means one thing only, literature a controlled suggestion of multiple extensions beyond the apparent sense of the statement, with a consequently greater faithfulness to the complexity of total states of mind.

Discuss whether this view of the use of language in literature agrees with that of Mr Bernard Mayo referred to on page 31.

11. Four boys are examined in three different subjects and an order of merit is produced for all the subjects combined. Does this necessarily involve the use of a *Cardinal* as well as an *Ordinal* Scale? (See page 120.)

12. Comment on the following:

And it is just this same fact – the fact that, on any 'subjective' interpretation the very same kind of thing which, under some circumstances, is better than another, would, under others, be worse – which constitutes, so far as I can see, the fundamental objection to all 'subjective' interpretations. G. E. MOORE, 'The Conception of Intrinsic Value', in *Philosophical Studies*, pp. 256–7.

13. From Boswell's *Life of Dr Johnson*:

BOSWELL: A worthy carman will get to heaven as well as Sir Isaac Newton. Yet, though equally good, they will not have the same degree of happiness.
JOHNSON: Probably not.
[Boswell goes on to say:]
Upon this subject I had once before sounded him, by mentioning the late Reverend Mr Brown of Utrecht's image; that a great and small glass, though equally full did not hold an equal quantity; which he threw out to refute David Hume's saying, that a little miss, going to dance at a ball, in a fine new dress, was as happy as a great orator after having made an eloquent and applauded speech. After some thought, Johnson said, 'I come over to the Parson.' JAMES BOSWELL, *The Life of Dr Johnson*, Vol. II, p. 207.

Do you agree with the parson or with Hume?
Discuss.

14. *A thing is good insofar as it exemplifies its concept.*
   This means that (1) the thing has a certain name, (2) this

name has a meaning defined by a set of properties, and (3) the thing possesses all the properties contained in the meaning of the name. A chair is a good chair if it actually and sensibly has the properties that define the concept 'chair'. . . .

The absoluteness or relativity of value is an age-old question. Its resolution is very simple. The question is whether there is an absolute norm of value, that is, a universal measure, in comparison with which every other value is determined. The answer is, yes, there is. The universal norm of value for each thing is the thing's own name. Norm equals name. Whenever I judge a thing as to its value, I compare the meaning of its name with the properties of the thing itself. . . .

Is value objective or subjective. The answer again is very simple: The *axiom* of value is *objective*. It is valid for every rational being whatsoever. . . . Whenever a being thinks rationally, that is, combines concept with objects, then he will have a term in his language which connotes that a concept corresponds to an object and vice versa, and this is the term that in our languages is called 'good', '*bon*' . . . etc. Formal or axiological value thus is objective. But its *application is subjective*. It may well be possible that what I call good you call bad, and what I call bad you call good. But this is a matter of application of axiology and not of axiology itself. . . .

Whenever anybody thinks that a thing fulfils its definition he will call it good, and whenever he thinks it does not fulfil its definition he will call it bad, and thus he will confirm axiology. Whether he rightly or wrongly thinks that a thing fulfils its definition is a different question – not one of axiology but one of its application. R. S. HARTMAN, *Value Theory as a Formal System.* ('Axiology' is defined earlier in the article as the *science of value.*)

Discuss the view of value set out in these extracts. In particular consider the application of the view to a work of art – e.g. a picture.

Supplementary passages

Some quotations illustrating objective and subjective views of literary merit:

(1) i. 'What is the greatest work ever written in the English language? *Hamlet*.' PHILIP TOYNBEE, *Observer*, 8 January 1961.

ii. In a letter to the *Observer* a week later Dr F. R. Leavis writes '. . . he (Mr Toynbee) takes the category "great" seriously and seems to think he means something by calling *Hamlet* great'.

(2) The one thing I most emphatically do not ask of a critic is that he tells me what I *ought* to approve of or condemn. I have no objection to his telling me what works and authors he likes and dislikes. W. H. AUDEN, *The Dyer's Hand and Other Essays*.

This was quoted in the *Sunday Times* of 21 January 1963 by Raymond Mortimer, who went on to say:

Almost all readers will agree with this last excerpt. Critics cannot qualify their every judgement with the words 'I believe that' or 'in my view' (Mr Auden would never allow himself to be so tedious); but by their tone they can imply this qualification. If they display a wish to lay down the law they must be inexperienced, conceited or puritanical.

(3) In comparing the merits of different versions of some essays by D. H. Lawrence, the reviewer (D. J. Enright) writes:

To make these early versions available is one thing. To assert again and again that they are superior to the *Studies*, as Dr Arnold does, is another thing altogether: a great big untruth. *New Statesman*, 10 August 1962.

(4) 'I believe myself that books *are* good or bad: I am not a subjectivist.' PHILIP TOYNBEE, letter in *Encounter*, June 1960.

(5) The works I admired were what they clearly were, and the grounds of my admiration were such as I certainly hadn't put there myself . . . I see no possibility at all of questioning the nature and conditions of the value of these things. F. R. LEAVIS, *The Common Pursuit*, p. 231.

(6) The critic, one would suppose, if he is to justify his existence, should endeavour to discipline his personal prejudices and cranks – tares to which we are all subject – and compose his differences with as many of his fellows as possible in the common pursuit of true judgement. T. S. ELIOT, *The Function of Criticism*.

APPEARANCE AND REALITY

As we have already remarked the main occupation of scientists is to examine, analyse and explain the physical world they find around them. This physical world has been examined and thought about also in a rather less scientific way by philosophers.

The scientists have weighed and measured and come to conclusions which have been of great use to mankind in enabling them, to some extent at least, to control and make predictions about the natural world.

The philosophers have speculated and asked awkward questions about the basis of the knowledge with which the scientists were operating, about the validity of the *facts* which the scientists have taken for granted. We shall now examine in some detail the questions which the philosophers have asked and the speculations in which they have indulged and try to decide to what extent, if any, the questions are answerable and the speculations profitable.

In the early days of philosophical speculation there was much controversy about the possibility of what was called 'a priori' or innate knowledge, that is to say of knowledge with which one was born and which was not derived from experience. One was said to be born with the *potentiality* for knowledge rather than the knowledge itself, for obviously it would be hard to maintain and still harder to prove that a new-born infant *knew* anything very much in the ordinary sense of knowing.

But whether or not one agreed about the possibility of

any sort of 'a priori' knowledge there could hardly be serious disagreement with the claim that most of our knowledge of the external, physical world must come to us through our senses. It may come to us personally, directly, as when we 'know' that there are two chairs in this room because we are sitting in one and have our feet on the other. Or it may come to us in a sense indirectly as when we 'know' that England lost the Test Match against Australia which finished yesterday, because we read about it in the newspapers. In the second case we acquired the 'knowledge' through our eyes, not by seeing it happen, but by reading about it, but what we read was written, we hope and assume, by someone who was himself an eye-witness. In other words, all that mankind collectively 'knows' about the physical world is derived from the collective senses of mankind, though this 'knowledge' may be passed on from one individual to others.

It will have been noticed that in the preceding paragraph 'know' and 'knowledge' have been written, perhaps rather irritatingly, in inverted commas. This has been as a reminder that what we mean by 'knowing' in this context is at present under investigation, the concept of our knowledge of the external world is what we are examining, and one of the questions that is going to be asked is whether we really *know* this or whether it is all illusion.

We might also make the point at this stage that there have been extensive investigations recently into the possibilities of extra-sensory perception (E.S.P.), that is, acquiring knowledge of the external world by means other than perception through our normal five senses. Many people claim that the reality of this has already been convincingly established. If this is so, it will be interesting to see (though the question will be a 'merely verbal' one) whether the facts will be described by saying that the age-old claim that all our knowledge of the external world comes to us through our senses is now seen to be false, or by saying that there is another, sixth, sense.

For the moment we shall disregard this possibility, partly because we are describing what has been said and thought about the matter before the possibility of E.S.P. was mooted, and partly because it seems certainly true that at any rate a very large proportion of our knowledge comes to us through our five senses. How certain, how secure is this knowledge?

A common starting point in investigating this question is for the student to be asked to focus his attention on some ordinary physical object such as a penny and to consider what we really know about it.

Commonsense would think of it as a material thing possessing at any moment certain 'qualities' or 'properties' – brownness, roundness, coolness, hardness, smoothness; or describable by certain adjectives – brown, round, cool, etc. But it is easy to demonstrate how, in a sense, 'unreal' these properties seem to be, to what extent they are matters of appearance rather than of reality; how *relative* they are; how they depend on the observer; how, therefore, they are 'subjective' rather than 'objective'.

This is perhaps most obviously seen in the case of colour, and we cannot do better than quote the demonstration of this point by the man who is perhaps the most famous philosopher of the century, Bertrand Russell. In the first chapter of his book *The Problems of Philosophy* he is discussing a table:

Although I believe that the table is 'really' of the same colour all over, the parts that reflect the light look much brighter than the other parts, and some parts look white because of reflected light. I know that, if I move, the parts that reflect the light will be different, so that the apparent distribution of colours on the table will change. It follows that if several people are looking at the table at the same moment, no two of them will see exactly the same distribution of colours, because no two can see it from exactly the same point of view, and any change in the point of view makes some change in the way the light is reflected. . . . It is evident . . . that there is no colour which preeminently appears to be *the* colour of the table, or even of any one particular part of the table – it appears to be of different colours from different points of view, and there is no reason for regarding some of these as more really its colour than others. And we know that even from a given point of view the colour will seem different by artificial light, or to a colour-blind man, or to a man wearing blue spectacles, while in the dark there will be no colour at all, though to touch and hearing the table will be unchanged. This colour is not something which is inherent in the table, but something depending upon the table and the spectator and the way the light falls on the table. When, in ordinary life, we speak of *the* colour of the table, we only mean the sort of colour which it will seem to have to a normal spectator from an ordinary point of view under usual conditions of light. But the other colours which appear under other conditions have just as good a right to be considered real; and therefore to avoid favouritism, we are compelled to deny that in itself, the table has any one particular colour. Op. cit., pp. 8, 9, 10.

Russell then goes on to demonstrate that similar arguments apply to other qualities.

Even if we take what might be thought of as the fixed geometrical physical property of its rectangular shape we have to admit that it does in fact look different from different points of view, that the 'real' shape is not what we see; it is something inferred from what we see. And what we see is constantly changing in shape as we move about the room; so that here again the senses seem not to give us the truth about the table itself, but only about the appearance of the table. Op. cit., p. 11.

BERKELEY'S VIEWS ON THE EXTERNAL WORLD

Considerations of this kind led some philosophers, notably Bishop Berkeley (1685-1753), to doubt whether physical objects in the ordinarily accepted sense could be said to exist at all. It will be useful to take a look, by considering some quotations, at his line of thought. His views about these things were expounded mainly in his *Treatise Concerning the Principles of Human Knowledge* and his *Three Dialogues between Hylas and Philonous, in Opposition to Sceptics and Atheists.* He opens Part I of the *Principles* by propounding at once his main thesis:

I. *Objects of Human knowledge.* It is evident to anyone who takes a survey of the objects of human knowledge, that they are either *ideas* actually (1) imprinted on the senses, or else such as are (2) perceived by attending to the passions and operations of the mind, or lastly, ideas (3) formed by help of memory and imagination, either compounding, dividing or barely representing those originally perceived in the aforesaid ways. By sight I have the ideas of light and colours with their several degrees and variations. By touch I perceive, for example, hard and soft, heat and cold, motion and resistance, and of all these more or less either as to quantity or degree. Smelling furnishes me with odours; the palate with tastes; and hearing conveys sounds to the mind in all their variety of tone and composition. And as several of these are observed to accompany each other, they come to be marked by one name, and so to be reputed as one thing. Thus, for example, a certain colour, taste, smell, figure and consistence having been observed to go together, are accounted one distinct thing, signified by the name *apple*. Other collections of ideas constitute a stone, a tree, a book, and the like sensible things; which, as they are pleasing or disagreeable, excite the passions of love, hatred, joy, grief and so forth. BERKELEY, *Principles*, p. 113.

There is no difficulty in seeing what Berkeley means by his three-fold division of ideas. The ideas 'imprinted on the senses', or our sensations, have often been called by philosophers in more recent times 'sense-data'. There are secondly those ideas which we should call hopes or fears or desires or the like; and there are thirdly the ideas of remembering or imagining.

He goes on:

II. *Mind-spirit-soul*. But besides all that endless variety of ideas or objects of knowledge, there is likewise something which knows or perceives them, and exercises divers operations, as willing, imagining, remembering about them. This perceiving, active being is what I call *mind, spirit, soul* or *myself*. By which words I do not denote any one of my ideas, but a thing entirely distinct from them, *wherein they exist*, or, which is the same thing, whereby they are perceived; for the existence of an idea consists in being perceived. . . .

As to what is said of the absolute existence of unthinking things without any relation to their being perceived, that seems perfectly unintelligible. Their *esse* is *percipi*, nor is it possible they should have any existence, out of the minds or thinking things which perceive them.

IV. *The vulgar opinion involves a contradiction*. It is indeed an opinion *strangely* prevailing amongst men, that houses, mounttains, rivers, and in a word all sensible objects have an existence natural or real, distinct from their being perceived by the understanding. But with how great an assurance and acquiescence soever this principle may be entertained in the world; yet whoever shall find in his heart to call it in question, may, if I mistake not, perceive it to involve a manifest contradiction.

For what are the forementioned objects but the things we *perceive* by sense, and what do we perceive *besides our own ideas or sensations;* and is it not plainly repugnant that any one of these or any combination of them should exist unperceived? V. *Cause of this prevalent error.* If we thoroughly examine this tenet, it will, perhaps, be found at bottom to depend on the doctrine of *abstract ideas.* For can there be a nicer strain of abstraction than to distinguish the existence of sensible objects from their being perceived, so as to conceive them existing unperceived? Light and colours, heat and cold, extension and figures, in a word the things we see and feel, what are they but so many sensations, notions, ideas, or impressions on the sense; and is it possible to separate, even in thought, any of these from perception? For my part I might as easily divide a thing from itself. . . . Hence as it is impossible for me to see or feel anything without an actual sensation of that thing, so it is impossible for me to conceive in my thoughts any sensible thing or object distinct from the sensation or perception of it. Op. cit., pp. 113–15.

We shall discuss later what he calls the doctrine of abstract ideas, and consider the effect it had on his thinking. It is not difficult, however, to grasp his main point; all that we know is our sense-data at the moment of our experiencing them: what reason have we for supposing that they, or anything else that is somehow related to them, have any existence apart from our experience. All that we know as we sip the nectar is the sweetness of the taste. What reason have we for supposing that the taste has any existence apart from our experience? Or indeed does it make any sense to talk or think about the taste existing apart from our experience?

He proceeds with what has become a particularly famous and much quoted paragraph:

VI. Some truths there are so near and obvious to the mind, that a man need only open his eyes to see them. Such I take this important one to be, to wit, that all the choir of heaven and furniture of the earth, in a word all those bodies which compose the mighty frame of the world, have not any subsistence without a mind, that their *being (esse)* is to be perceived or known; that consequently so long as they are not actually perceived by me, or do not exist in my mind or that of any other *created spirit*, they must either have no existence at all, *or else subsist in the mind of some eternal spirit:* it being perfectly unintelligible and involving all the absurdity of abstraction, to attribute to any single part of them an existence independent of a spirit. To be convinced of which, the reader need only reflect and try to separate in his own thoughts the being of a sensible thing from its being perceived. Op. cit., pp. 115–16.

With this view of his that physical objects were, in a sense, a myth there would obviously also go the view that matter, which was often thought of as a permanent, objective substance which possessed the subjective, shifting, relative qualities, was a myth also.

By *matter* therefore we are to understand an inert, senseless substance, in which extension, figure and motion, *do actually subsist.* But it is evident from what we have already shown, that extension, figure and motion, are *only ideas existing in the mind*, and that an idea can be like nothing but another idea, and that consequently neither they not their archetypes can exist in an *unperceiving* substance. Hence it is plain, that the very notion of what is called *matter*, or *corporeal substance*, involves a contradiction in it. Op. cit., p. 117.

And again, a later paragraph runs:

I do not argue against the existence of any one thing that we can apprehend, either by sense or reflection. That the things I see with mine eyes and touch with my hands do exist, really exist, I make not the least question. The only thing whose existence we deny, *is that which philosophers call matter* or corporeal substance. Op. cit., p. 129.

It may be thought that in this last paragraph when he says that 'the things I see ... do ... really exist' he is contradicting what has gone before. It is quite clear in the context however that by 'things' he means 'ideas' and that these exist in and only in a mind. Matter however is not an idea and therefore cannot exist.

It is to be hoped that the above quotations will make it reasonably clear what Berkeley's views were. They were certainly startling to common sense – a point which is perhaps made even more forcibly in the *Dialogues* where Philonous represents Berkeley and Hylas the ordinary man. Hylas's initial reaction to what he has heard of Philonous's views was to say:

You were represented in last night's conversation as one who maintained the most extravagant opinion that ever entered into the mind of man, to wit, that there is no such thing as *material* substance in the world. *First Dialogue*, p. 200.

Berkeley's 'extravagant opinions' have been the subject of much ridicule and much misunderstanding. The common-sense reaction is well exemplified by Dr Johnson's answer as recounted by Boswell:

After we came out of church we stood talking for some time together of Bishop Berkeley's ingenious sophistry to prove the non-existence of matter and that everything in the universe is merely ideal. I observed, that though we are satisfied his doctrine is not true, it is impossible to refute it. I shall never forget the alacrity with which Johnson answered, striking his foot with mighty force against a large stone, till he rebounded from it, 'I refute it *thus*'.

Anyone who reads Berkeley at any length at all can be left in no doubt about the strength of his convictions, the certainty with which he thought that his was the right, and indeed the only possible view, and that anyone who had the truth pointed out to him and took the trouble to reflect upon it could not fail to agree with him.

It is clearly important that we should be sure that we understand just what it was that Berkeley found unsatisfactory and puzzling about the ordinary common-sense view, that we should see the problem that he felt he was solving.

Berkeley concentrated his attention on the facts of experience and he certainly renders a service by reminding us of what is on reflection obvious, that all we know of the world around us comes to us through our senses. We *know* in the most direct and convincing way possible about the ideas of sensation, or the sense-data, that we have, the ideas of seeing, hearing, feeling. What is puzzling however is that the so-called external object 'out there', the thing that common sense thinks of as being responsible for the sensations that we have, seems consistently to elude our grasp. If we ask or think what it is, or what it is really like, any answers seem bound to be in terms of what it looks like or feels like, in other words in terms of just those sensations or ideas that we are trying to get behind. It is true, of course, that the answer which the scientist would give today to the question what it is really like, would be rather different, and would in a sense go deeper than would have been the case in Berkeley's day. And it is interesting that many of the things that modern scientists say provide support for Berkeley's point of view. In an essay on 'The Nature of Scientific Philosophy' Professor Herbert Dingle points out that it is not the world of material objects but experiences themselves which are the fundamental data of science. Material objects, he says, should be regarded by the scientist merely as conceptions which it is useful to postulate for certain purposes.

The peculiar characteristic of scientific philosophy, then, may be expressed in this way. Like all philosophy, its aim is to organize the whole of experience into a rationally connected system, but, unlike all previous philosophies, it does not accept the world of material objects, located and moving in a unique space and time, as a necessary starting point, but goes back to the original experiences that led to the conception of that world for practical ends, and groups them differently. H. DINGLE, *The Scientific Adventure*, pp. 203–4.

This seems to make in a rather more sophisticated way the same point that Berkeley was making. It may be useful to postulate 'apple' as a name for a group of experiences which are found together, but to go on from there to suppose that external objects exist 'out there' apart from our sensations is a very different matter.

The line of Berkeley's thought about this is best seen by quoting a complete paragraph:

XVIII. *The existence of external bodies wants proof*. But though it were possible that solid, figured, moveable substances may exist without the mind, corresponding to the ideas we have of bodies, *yet how is it possible for us to know this?* either we must know it by sense or by reason. As for our senses, by them we have the knowledge only of our *sensations*, ideas, or those things that are immediately perceived by sense, call them what you will: but they do not inform us that things exist without the mind, or unperceived, like to those which are perceived. This the materialists themselves acknowledge. It remains therefore that if we have any knowledge at all of external things, it must be by *reason*, inferring their existence from what is immediately perceived by sense. But I do not see what reason can induce us to believe the existence of bodies without the mind, from what we perceive, since the very patrons of matter themselves do not pretend, there is *any necessary connection betwixt them and our ideas*. I say, it is granted on all hands (and what happens in dreams, frenzies, and the like, puts it beyond dispute) that *it is possible we might be affected with all the ideas we have now, though no bodies existed without, resembling them.* Hence it is evident the supposition of external bodies is not necessary for producing our ideas; since it is granted they are produced sometimes, and might possibly be produced always, in the same order we see them in at present, without their concurrence. *Principles*, p. 121.

And at the end of the following paragraph he says:

If therefore it were possible for bodies to exist without the mind, yet to hold they do so must be a very precarious opinion; since it is to suppose, without any reason at all, that God has created innumerable beings *that are entirely useless, and serve to no manner of purpose. Principles*, p. 122.

Since then, there can be no proof of their existence, or as Berkeley would put it more strongly no reason to suppose that they exist, or no meaning to be attached to a statement of their existence ('the absolute existence of unthinking things are words without a meaning'), the simplest and indeed the only course is to deny their separate existence. Or to put it in another way the object just *is* the name we give to a certain collection of ideas or sensations, but it is nothing else in itself apart from these ideas. As Berkeley said in the first paragraph we quoted above 'A certain colour, taste, smell, figure and consistence having been observed to go together are accounted one direct thing, signified by the name *apple*.'

And, again, 'In truth the object and the sensation are the same thing, and cannot therefore be abstracted from each other.' *Principles V*, p. 115.

It is a fairly obvious corollary that, as we have seen from the passages quoted above, Berkeley also denied the exist-ence of matter, that is of 'an inert, senseless substance in which extension, figure, motion do actually subsist.' This notion would in any case hardly seem scientifically tenable today, but it is interesting that Berkeley abolished it for reasons rather different from those that we might expect. This matter was thought of by earlier philosophers as the 'substratum' which 'supported' qualities such as extension. If one abstracted or took away from matter all these qualities, such as colour, hardness, extension, it might well be asked what could possibly be left; it could, by definition, be nothing that could be sensed or perceived. As 'matter' in this sense therefore is unknown and unknowable it would seem reasonable to suggest that it was not a useful postulate and had better be abandoned. If *esse* is *percipi*, to suppose the existence of something that could by definition not be perceived would seem to involve a contradiction.

Berkeley however abolished matter not because it could not *be* perceived but because it could not perceive. Matter was supposed to be an inert, senseless substance in which extension etc. subsisted. But since extension and other qualities are only ideas, and since ideas can only exist in a mind or a perceiving substance, matter which is thought of as an unperceiving substance cannot support or possess ideas or qualities. Existence therefore is denied to matter here not because '*esse*' is '*percipi*' but because it is '*percipere*'; because, in Berkeley's words again, 'there is not any other substance than spirit or that which perceives'. (This is not to say of course that nothing exists except spirit, there are also the ideas which spirits have, but their existence is relative and dependent on the existence of the spirits.)

BERKELEY AND GOD

The spirits however are not only human spirits. There is

also God, who played, not unnaturally, a very important part in Berkeley's scheme of things. To the objection that his principles would involve 'perpetual annihilation and creation', that 'the objects of sense exist only when they are perceived', that 'upon shutting my eyes all the furniture in the room is reduced to nothing and barely upon opening them it is again created' (*Principles XLV*, p. 134), he answered in the first place by asking the reader to consider again 'whether he means anything by the actual existence . of an idea, distinct from its being perceived' (*Principles XLV*, p. 134). In other words he sticks to his point and his thesis that to exist consists in being perceived, with the implication that any puzzlement about perpetual annihilation and creation is derived from the other sense of existence the orthodox, common-sense view; to raise this objection against Berkeley is to miss the point and beg the question. And it is in a similar way that Dr Johnson's 'refutation' misses the point and begs the question.

Berkeley, however, also has a second line of defence to the perpetual annihiliaton objection. In the Second Dialogue Philonous says:

To me it is evident . . . that sensible things cannot exist otherwise than in a mind or spirit. Whence I conclude, not that they have no real existence, but that seeing they depend not on my thought, and have an existence distinct from being perceived by me, *there must be some other mind wherein they exist*. As sure, therefore, as the sensible world really exists, so sure is there an infinite, omnipresent Spirit who contains and supports it. *Dialogues*, p. 245.

In other words, things go on existing even when no human being is perceiving them because everything is always perceived by God, or is an idea in his mind.

This theory of Berkeley's is summed up in a limerick by Ronald Knox and the reply to it:

> There was a young man who said, 'God
> Must think it exceedingly odd
>   If he finds that this tree
>   Continues to be
> When there's no one about in the Quad.'

> 'Dear Sir,
>   Your astonishment's odd:
> I am always about in the Quad.
>   And that's why the tree
>   Will continue to be,
>   Since observed by
>   Yours faithfully,
>   God.'

It is interesting that Philonous goes on to say:

Men commonly believe that all things are known or perceived by God, because they believe the being of a God, whereas I, on the other side, immediately and necessarily conclude the being of a God, because all sensible things must be perceived by him. *Dialogues*, p. 245.

The feeling therefore that God is needed to ensure the existence of all things when no human mind is perceiving them ('if they really exist, they are necessarily perceived by an infinite mind') is used as a proof of the existence of God ('therefore there is an infinite mind, or God'). (*Dialogues*, p. 246.)

Another important function of God in Berkeley's theory was to distinguish between ideas of sensation and what he called ideas of reflection, that is the ideas which we have when we are imagining things, seeing things in our mind's eyes, remembering how things looked, or sounded or tasted. The distinction which common sense would make between the ideas of sensation and reflection would be that in the one case there is a material object 'out there' causing the sensation and that in the other case there is not. This course however is obviously not open to Berkeley. He sees that the ideas of reflection and memory can be manipulated at will but not the ideas of sensation. 'There is therefore some other will or spirit that produces them' (*Principles XXIX*, p. 127); they are 'imprinted on the senses by the author of nature'.

The ideas of sense are allowed to have more reality in them ... that is, to be more (1) strong, (2) orderly and (3) coherent, than the creatures of the mind; but this is no argument that they exist without the mind. They are also (4) less dependent on the spirit, or thinking substance which perceives them, in that they are excited by the will of another and more powerful spirit. *Principles XXXIII*, p. 128.

Furthermore, says Berkeley, from this superiority of ideas of sensation to those of reflection other conclusions can be drawn: 'There is a mind which affects me every moment with all the sensible impressions I perceive. And from the variety, order and manner of these, I conclude the author of them to be wise, powerful, and good, beyond comprehension.' (*Second Dialogue*, p. 249.) And again, 'The order of our perception shows the goodness of God, but affords no proof of the existence of matter.' (*Principles LXXII*, p. 149.)

Such then was Berkeley's theory. For him the only realities were spiritual substances or minds and the ideas which these minds had. What we call objects are merely collections of ideas. The supreme mind of God in a sense ensures the continuity of these objects by having the ideas which constitute them when no other mind is having them.

God is also responsible for the order and coherence of the ideas of sensation which we human minds experience. This philosophical theory is called 'Subjective Idealism' ('Idealism' in this context of course means the -ism connected with *ideas* and not that connected with *ideals*.)

HUME'S DEVELOPMENT OF SUBJECTIVE IDEALISM

Before we attempt to criticize Berkeley's views in detail it will be interesting and useful to consider briefly how they were developed by the British philosopher who is usually thought of as Berkeley's successor, namely David Hume (1711–76).

Hume wrote widely on many topics; for the moment we are interested mainly in what he had to say about the existence of physical objects. His methods of philosophizing and what he wrote were of very considerable importance. Sir Isaiah Berlin says of him 'No man has influenced the history of philosophical thought to a deeper and more disturbing degree.' (*The Age of Enlightenment*, p. 163.)

Like Berkeley, Hume based his inquiry on the facts of experience, our sensations or ideas. Where Berkeley distinguished between ideas of sensation and ideas of reflection, Hume distinguished between *impressions* and *ideas*. 'The difference,' he says, 'betwixt these consists in the degrees of force and liveliness, with which they strike upon the mind, and make their way into our thought or consciousness.' (DAVID HUME, *A Treatise of Human Nature*, I.I.I.) It is the difference between *feeling* and *thinking*. In general they are easily distinguishable,

but, in particular instances they may very nearly approach to each other. Thus in sleep, in a fever, in madness, or in any very violent emotions of soul, our ideas may approach to our impressions: as, on the other hand, it sometimes happens that our impressions are so faint and low that we cannot distinguish them from our ideas.

It is then an obvious question to ask whether there exist material bodies which are separate from these impressions and which in some sense are responsible for them or cause them. Hume, who pursued a sceptical, doubting method more thoroughly perhaps than any other philosopher before or since, regarded material objects as an illusion or fiction whose reality could certainly not be proved, but whose existence in a sense it might be convenient to assume.

. . . the sceptic . . . must assent to the principle concerning the existence of body, though he cannot pretend, by any arguments of philosophy, to maintain its veracity. Nature has not left this to his choice and has doubtless esteemed it an affair of too great importance to be trusted to our uncertain reasonings and speculations. We may well ask *What causes induce us to believe in the existence of body?* but it is in vain to ask, *Whether there be body or not?* That is a point which we must take for granted in all our reasonings. Op. cit., I. IV. 2.

He then goes on to consider the other, psychological question as to why in fact we *do* believe – and in their common-sense moments mankind would be almost unanimous in so doing – in the *continued* and *independent* existence of material bodies. He says:

Our reason neither does, not is it possible it ever should, upon any supposition give us an assurance of the continued and distinct existence of body. That opinion must be entirely owing to the *imagination*. Op. cit., I. I. 2, p. 188.

He goes on to say that we form 'the opinion of the continued existence of body' because of 'the *coherence* and constancy of certain impressions'. 'I now proceed,' he continues, 'to examine after what manner these qualities give rise to so extraordinary an opinion.' (Op cit., I. 1. 2.)

In this examination he describes ordinary commonplace ways in which our sensations or impressions of what we might call a material object fit in with each other or cohere. Common-sense would certainly say that this coherence between, for example, our visual impression and our sensation of touch would be a main test that we apply to determine whether a table is 'really there' or not. Another test we might apply if we are wondering whether the table is imaginary would be to shut our eyes for a bit and see if it is still there when we open them again; in other words, to see whether the impressions are constant.

There is scarce a moment of my life wherein . . . I have not occasion to suppose the continued existence of objects, in order to connect their past and present appearances, and give them such a union with each other, as I have found, by experience, to be suitable to their particular natures and circumstances. Here, then, I am naturally led to regard the world as something real and durable, and as preserving its existence even when it is no longer present to my perception . . . Op. cit., I. IV. 2.

But though this is how he is 'led to regard the world', he does not consider that any sort of proof has been provided. He is merely describing reasons why we do in fact form 'so extraordinary an opinion'.

Hume was an atheist and for him therefore there was no Berkeleyan God whose mind could entertain the ideas of sensation and thus ensure their continued existence. Worse than that, however, not only was there no divine mind, but also when he came to examine the concept of the individual mind, the notion of the self, it proved to be, like the independent material object, exceedingly elusive.

When I enter most intimately into what I call *myself*, I always stumble on some particular perception or other, of heat or cold, light or shade, love or hatred, pain or pleasure. I never catch *myself* at any time without a perception, and never can observe anything but the perception. When my perceptions are removed for any time, as by sound sleep, so long am I insensible of *myself*, and may truly be said not to exist. And were all my perceptions removed by death, and could I neither think, nor feel, nor see, nor love, nor hate, after the dissolution of my body, I should be entirely annihilated, nor do I conceive what is farther requisite to make me a perfect nonentity. If any one, upon serious and unprejudiced reflection, thinks he has a different notion of *himself*, I must confess I can reason no longer with him. All I can allow him is, that he may be in the right as well as I, and that we are essentially different in this particular. He may, perhaps, perceive something simple and continued, which he calls *himself;* though I am certain there is no such principle in me.

But setting aside some metaphysicians of this kind, I may venture to affirm of the rest of mankind that they are nothing but a bundle or collection of different perceptions, which succeed each other with an inconceivable rapidity, and are in a perpetual flux and movement. Op. cit., I. iv. 6.

For Hume therefore the only entities of whose existence there can be certainty are 'particular perceptions'. It does not even make sense to say 'of which we are certain' for there is no 'we' to feel certain. He is unable to find a 'principle of connexion', which binds the particular perceptions together, either in the material object which common sense supposes to bind a particular group of cohering perceptions together, or in a mind or a self which common sense supposes to 'have' a particular group of perceptions. This is the view of extreme scepticism, that nothing is real except particular perceptions. It is called Solipsism, and it is usually thought of as the logical conclusion of Subjective Idealism, the blind alley into which that line of inquiry takes us. It is not surprising that Hume, who was a modest man and was described by Adam Smith as 'approaching as nearly to the idea of a perfectly wise and virtuous man as perhaps the nature of human frailty will admit', was not exactly satisfied with the results or rather, in some senses, the lack of results of his speculations. 'I am sensible,' he says, 'that my account is very defective', and towards the end of the Appendix to the Treatise of Human Nature come the words:

For my part I must plead the privilege of a sceptic, and confess that this difficulty is too hard for my understanding. I pretend not, however, to pronounce it absolutely insuperable. Others, perhaps, or myself upon more mature reflections, may discover some hypothesis, that will reconcile these contradictions.

And not only was he unhappy about the conclusions to which his reasoning led him; in a sense, and in certain moods, he neither believed in them himself nor expected other people to:

This sceptical doubt, both with respect to reason and the senses is a malady which can never be radically cured, but must return upon us every moment, however we may chase it away, and sometimes may seem entirely free from it. It is impossible, upon any system, to defend either our understanding or senses; and we but expose them further when we endeavour to justify them in that manner. As the sceptical doubt arises naturally from a profound and intense reflection on those subjects, it always increases the farther we carry our reflections, whether in opposition or conformity to it. Carelessness and inattention alone can afford us any remedy. For this reason I rely entirely upon them: and take it for granted, whatever may be the reader's opinion at this present moment, that an hour hence he will be persuaded there is both an external and internal world. Op. cit., I. IV. 2.

THE VIEWS OF BERKELEY AND HUME CONSIDERED

It is unlikely that anyone who is reading this thinks at this stage that either Berkeley or Hume was right. But it is certainly not very obvious why they were wrong and not very likely that any reader will claim to have discovered 'some hypothesis that will reconcile those contradictions' of which Hume spoke.

It might be said that Hume makes us less disposed to believe Berkeley, not rationally or logically, but in the sense that if what Berkeley said is true then there seems no reason why one should not follow the logical train further and arrive at Hume's conclusions. These however really *can't* be true and there must surely therefore have been something wrong with Berkeley's theory, with his assumptions, his methods of arguing, or with his whole line of thought. It certainly seems to be the case that, as Bertrand Russell has said,

Hume's philosophy, whether true or false, represents the bankruptcy of eighteenth-century reasonableness. He starts out . . . with the intention of being sensible and empirical, taking nothing on trust, but seeking whatever instruction is to be obtained from experience and observation. But . . . he arrives at the disastrous conclusion that from experience and observation nothing is to be learnt. *History of Western Philosophy*, p. 698.

Let us then, before we examine Hume's findings further, take another look at what Berkeley had to say.

It will be remembered that Berkeley regarded as real only spiritual substance or mind and the ideas which minds have. There was no such thing for him as material substance, and the so-called objects were merely collections of ideas. For him *esse* was either *percipi* (the ideas) or *percipere* (minds): there was no sense in saying that an idea existed if no one was having it, and no sense in which one could say that a mind existed if it was not perceiving. As well as the minds of human beings there was also the mind of God which maintained all ideas in existence by having them, and was also responsible for the order and coherence of human ideas.

It will be convenient first, as one can do so swiftly, to dispose of two points: the first a portion of Berkeley's theory which is obviously unsatisfactory, the second a line of attack on him which is also obviously unsatisfactory.

Readers can hardly fail to have been struck by the obvious circularity of Berkeley's arguments about God. He explains, in one version of his views, the continued existence of ideas and their order and coherence by saying that God is responsible for these things, but he also uses the 'fact' that God does this as a proof of the existence and of the goodness of God.

The second point to be disposed of as a preliminary is what might be called the Dr Johnson, man-in-the-street, refutation of Berkeley. When Dr Johnson kicked the stone there was added an idea, no doubt a particularly vivid and perhaps a painful one, of feeling sensation to the ideas that he probably already had of visual sensation. For Berkeley it would clearly be no different in kind, and the only point that Dr Johnson may be considered to have made is that the ordinary man does in fact have a very strong conviction that ordinary objects do exist 'out there' and that Berkeley's explanation or description does not fit the facts. It was to overcome this conviction, which though it might not be an argument was certainly an important piece of evidence, that Berkeley reiterated his central principle again and again in his writings. For him it seemed to be intuitively obvious, a 'revolt from metaphysical notions to the plain dictates of nature and common sense' (*First Dialogue*, p. 200); but, unfortunately, to Dr Johnson and most other people it seemed just the reverse.

The easiest approach to a criticism of Berkeley's theory will be by taking a leaf out of Hume's book as far as method is concerned. It will be remembered that at one stage he thought it more profitable to consider what causes induced us to hold a certain belief than whether that belief was itself true. Let us similarly consider first *why* Berkeley thought as he did.

THE EFFECT OF LOCKE ON BERKELEY'S THOUGHT

We have not as yet mentioned that an important predecessor of Berkeley was John Locke (1623-1704). In the Introduction to his *Principles* Berkeley is concerned mainly to refute a particular doctrine of Locke's, that of abstract ideas. This doctrine was of old standing and derived particularly from Plato. Let us, briefly, take a look at it.

We have our particular perceptions or sensations and we use various adjectives about them such as red, hard, cold, round, long etc. Whether we think of these adjectives, as describing material objects 'out there' or, with Berkeley, as describing our ideas does not for the moment matter. It is convenient for various purposes to refer to what might be thought of as the property which various red objects have in common, and this is called 'redness'. Similarly other general words, 'coldness', 'roundness', 'length' etc. are coined. These general properties have sometimes been called universals and they have been thought to have an existence apart from particular red, cold, round objects. Plato, as we have already mentioned, regarded these universals or forms as more real than the particular objects, and thought of them as occupying the world of reality which was very different from the shadowy world of appearances. Beautiful red beds would become more real the more fully they participated in or represented the eternal, essential forms of beauty, redness and bed.

This theory, that universals in some sense exist, or as it is sometimes said 'subsist', apart from the particular objects in which they are exemplified is one that has been held in a less extreme form considerably more recently than Plato. For the moment what is relevant to our purposes is to consider what Berkeley had to say about Locke's notion of abstract ideas. Locke did not think, as Plato did, that the universals or forms existed in a more real world and this view does not seem to have been current when Berkeley was writing. 'It is agreed on all hands,' he says 'that the qualities or modes of things do never really exist each of them apart by itself' (*Principles*, p. 95), and he represents the view that he is attacking thus: 'Not that it is possible for colour or motion to exist without extension: but only that the mind can frame to itself by *abstraction* the idea of colour exclusive of extension, and of motion exclusive of both colour and extension' (op. cit., p. 96). Locke thought that this having of general ideas, this power of abstraction, was 'that which puts a perfect distinction betwixt men and brutes, and is an excellency which the faculties of brutes do by no means attain unto'. (Quoted by BERKELEY, op. cit., p. 99.) Berkeley however maintained that as a matter of introspection and experience he was not able to form the idea of whiteness apart from particular white objects, and even less the 'idea of colour in abstract, which is neither red nor blue, nor white, nor any other determinate colour.'

I can imagine a man with two heads, or the upper parts of a man joined to the body of a horse. I can consider the hand, the eye, the nose, each by itself abstracted or separated from the rest of the body. But then whatever hand or eye I imagine, it must have some particular shape and colour. Likewise the idea of man that I frame to myself, must be either of a white, or a black, or a tawny, a straight, or a crooked, a tall, or a low, or a middle-sized man. I cannot by any effort of thought conceive the abstract idea above described. And it is equally impossible for me to form the abstract idea of motion distinct from the body moving, and which is neither swift nor slow, curvilinear nor rectilinear and the like may be said of all other abstract general ideas whatsoever. Op. cit., p. 98.

He goes on to agree with Locke 'that the faculties of brutes can by no means attain to abstraction', and then continues rather acidly, 'But then if this be made the distinguishing property of that sort of animals, I fear a great many of those that pass for men must be reckoned into their number.' Op cit., p. 99.

Berkeley admits the existence of general ideas, but says that they owe their generality to 'being made to represent and stand for all other particular ideas of the same sort'. The general word 'line' stands for all particular lines, but there is no idea of an abstract general line apart from that. There are mainly particular white objects or examples of whiteness but there is no abstract general idea of whiteness.

Berkeley's argument against the existence of abstract general ideas was mainly an appeal to experience:

If any man has the faculty of forming in his mind such an idea of a triangle as is here described ('neither oblique, nor rectangle, neither equilateral, equicrural nor scalenon, but all and none of these at once'), it is in vain to pretend to dispute him out of it, nor would I go about it. All I desire is that the reader would fully and certainly inform himself whether he has such an idea or no. Op. cit., p. 102.

He also denied, in opposition to Locke, that they made communication more convenient or helped to enlarge our knowledge. Not only were they an unjustifiable hypothesis, but also a useless one. He considered that the source of this mistake was language and the errors and misunderstandings that arose from its improper use.

Most parts of knowledge have been strangely perplexed and darkened by the abuse of words and general ways of speech wherein they are delivered. Since therefore, words are so apt to impose on the understanding, whatever ideas I consider, I shall endeavour to take them bare and naked into my view, keeping out of my thoughts, so far as I am able, those names which long and constant use hath so strictly united with them; . . . Op. cit., p. 109.

(It is interesting that in the first, 1710, edition he added: 'I am resolved in my inquiries to make as little use of them as possibly I can.' One wonders whether this sentence was removed because of the difficulties he experienced in speculating without words, or because of the obvious fact that as it was his intention to communicate the results of his speculations they had inevitably to be described in words eventually.)

It might be said that the abstract idea as Locke described it was not an idea at all in the main sense that Berkeley used the word, in the sense, that is to say, of an idea of sensation derived from experience, because it was not something of which the mind could be immediately aware. For Berkeley therefore it was nothing; merely a myth deriving from an improper use of words.

It has been suggested by G. J. Warnock (*Berkeley*) that it was partly as a result of what Berkeley felt to have been his successful attack on this aspect of Locke's philosophy that he fell into error in other ways.

He saw the doctrine of false abstraction, 'a chief source of error in all parts of knowledge', as responsible for the unjustifiable and useless hypothesis of abstract ideas. Locke believed in the existence of material substances or objects. He did not think that they were directly perceptible or knowable by us. All we could know were ideas. But he thought that they *caused* the ideas that we have of them. It seemed to Berkeley however that this hypothesis was analogous to that of abstract ideas and was similarly unjustifiable and useless.

Can there be a nicer strain of abstraction than to distinguish the existence of sensible objects from their being perceived, so as to conceive them existing unperceived. Light and colours, heat and cold, extension and figures – in a word, the things we see and feel – what are they but so many sensations, notions, ideas, or impressions on the sense ? And is it possible to separate, even in thought, any of these from perception ? Op. cit., p. 115.

Berkeley claims, and most philosophers would now say rightly claims, that it does not make sense to talk, for example, of motion existing apart from moving objects. There are certainly many useful general remarks one might make using the word 'motion', but these remarks can only apply to moving objects, perhaps many of them, perhaps all of them. If we try to find motion or the idea of motion separated from moving things we are doomed to disappointment. He goes on, however, to say or imply that just as the word 'motion' can only apply to particular examples of things moving, and the general word 'line' can only mean the sum of particular lines, so also the word 'table' when applied to what would normally be regarded as a particular object can only mean the collection of particular ideas or sensations that we have of it. It is illegitimate, says Berkeley, to claim that we can abstract the general idea of redness from particular ideas of red and to suppose that 'redness' in some sense exists in its own right. So also it seemed to him illegitimate to abstract from our ideas or sensations and to suppose that there is any sense in which 'apple' exists apart from the 'certain colour, taste, smell, figure and consistence' which have been observed to go together.

There is no implication here that Berkeley was falsely arguing by analogy, but simply the suggestion that this comparison, this line of thought, led him to believe as he did. The material objects of Locke which were unknown and unknowable and which caused our ideas were obviously unsatisfactory; so too were the abstract general ideas which he found by introspection he could not form. The thesis that the general word stood merely for a host of particular examples, disposed of the latter theory, it was not surprising that he was led to think that a similar argument would dispose of the former.

There are, however, important differences. We look for redness apart from red objects and we cannot find it, we look for table apart from our perceptions of it and we cannot find that either. So far there is a superficial similarity. Berkeley's contention that there are no such things as abstract general ideas is supported by an appeal to our introspective experience. Many people however have certainly claimed, as Locke did, that they *can* form a general idea of redness apart from particular red objects: they might admit under a persuasive cross-examination that they are wrong, that their idea is just of rather a vague, indeterminate, particular red mass, but it is certainly a matter about which there is room for differences of opinion. Berkeley's similar disposal of material objects however is on a different footing: he makes his case irrefutable by the way he states it; he states it as a tautology.

What he is claiming is that if we look for the material object, 'table', apart from our sensations or perceptions, it eludes our grasp or thought; that we can't form an idea of a table apart from our ideas of it, and this of course is to state the proposition in such a way that we are bound to say 'Of course we can't'. If our 'idea' of it is not allowed to be what it looks like, feels like, smells like etc. of course we can form no conception of it. For in what other terms is it possible for us to form a conception of it?

AMBIGUITY OF 'IDEAS'

Closely bound up with this criticism of Berkeley is the point made against him by many commentators that there is a question-begging ambiguity in his use of the word 'idea'. It is said that he used it to apply both to the objects of sensation or experience and to the acts of seeing or experiencing; both to the things and to our ideas of sensation of these things.

What Berkeley himself says about this is important and relevant:

But, say you, it sounds very harsh to say we eat and drink ideas, and are clothed with ideas. I acknowledge it does so, the word *idea* not being used in common discourse to signify the several qualities, which are called *things*: and it is certain that any expression which varies from the familiar use of language, will seem harsh and ridiculous. But this doth not concern the truth of the proposition, which in other words is no more than to say, we are fed and clothed with these things which we perceive immediately by our senses. The hardness or softness, the colour, taste, warmth, figure and such like qualities, which combined together constitute the several sorts of victuals and apparel, have been shown to exist only in the mind that perceives them: and this is all that is meant by calling them *ideas;* which word, if it was as ordinarily used as *thing*, would sound no harsher nor more ridiculous than it. I am not for disputing about the propriety, but the truth of the expression. If therefore you agree with me that we eat, and drink, and are clad with the immediate objects of sense, which cannot exist unperceived or without the mind; I shall readily grant it is more proper or conformable to custom, that they should be called things rather than ideas. *Principles* XXXVIII, p. 131.

It is clear from this that the reason why Berkeley refrains from calling the objects of sensation and the act of sensing by different names (things and ideas) is simply that he does not think they are different. His whole theory is that the 'combinations of sensible qualities which are called things' ... exist only in the mind that perceives them and should therefore more properly be called ideas.

It does not therefore seem plausible to suggest that Berkeley was himself misled or bewitched by the undoubted fact that he used the word 'ideas' to apply to what those who disagreed with him would regard as separate entities. But it might certainly be felt that there was a possibility of his misleading others by doing this in his arguments. To pursue an analogy similar to one that we used in an earlier chapter, if we are quite sure that two personalities whom we have met in different contexts, say the postman and the centre-forward of the village football team, are really the same man, it will be perfectly reasonable for us to call them by the same name. There will only have been a bewitchment if we think they are the same *because* or partly because they have the same name. It does not seem that Berkeley came to think that sensations and the objects of sensation were really the same *because* he or anyone else had attached the same name to them; but rather he attached the same name to them *because* he thought they were the same.

On the other hand someone who thinks that the postman and the centre-forward are different people and who is arguing with me about it might well say that my insistence in calling them by the same name begs the question; though I might equally well argue that his insistence on calling them different names begs the question the other way. Similarly it can certainly be claimed by someone who disagrees with Berkeley or is suspending judgement on the matter that his use of the word 'idea' in his arguments may on occasion appear to beg the question that he is trying to prove, and may therefore tend to mislead others though not himself.

(In the case of the postman and the centre-forward an obvious step to take to help resolve the argument would be to find out what their names in fact are. This would be an important and might be a conclusive piece of evidence. To take a similar step and make inquiries as to whether the acts of sensation and objects of sensation are in fact called by the same name would clearly be much more difficult without begging the question, and the evidence provided by the answers, though perhaps of some value, would be much less conclusive.)

MANY CRITICISMS OF BERKELEY VALID ALSO AGAINST HUME

We have considered criticisms of Berkeley's position rather

than of Hume's because, as we have already remarked, the second is so obviously the logical development and conclusion of the first. Hume applied to the mind and its acts of perceiving the same treatment as Berkeley applied to the object and the mind's perceptions of it. Just as it was an unjustifiable hypothesis and the result of a false abstraction to suppose that there was any material object apart from our perceptions, so there was no justification in supposing the existence of any mental entity other than particular acts of perception.

In spite of the ways in which Hume's thinking followed on from Berkeley's it is interesting to notice a particular very important difference between them. Berkeley saw himself as contending against sceptics and atheists and was quite sure he was right; it is hard to find any note of doubt in his writings. Hume, on the other hand was an atheist, and refers, as we have seen, at the conclusion of this Treatise to the scepticism to which his philosophy has led him. He also makes it quite clear that he does not think that *certainty* is to be attained as a result of the speculations in which he is engaged. It may well be, and we shall return to this later, that this is the most important point he makes.

PUZZLEMENT REMAINS

In spite of all that has been said the reader may well feel still, and perhaps should feel still, a residue of unresolved and dissatisfied puzzlement. However much we may disagree with their conclusions it may well be thought that the arguments of Berkeley and Hume have not been satisfactorily disposed of. It is Berkeley's great merit that he draws our attention again and again to the fact that all we immediately and directly know is our sense-experience. In an earlier chapter we spoke of the danger of supposing that because a word exists therefore the things which the word is supposed to represent must exist also. Many of our leading present-day thinkers sound this same warning insistently. Lord Brain, a leading expert on the human brain, talks of the confusion about the proper use of the words 'mind' and 'mental', and suggests that it 'might have been avoided if people had been content to speak in terms of human subjective experiences and behaviour rather than of hypothetical entities'. (*The Humanist Frame*, p. 54.) And surely if Berkeley had been alive to read that, he would have claimed that this was precisely what he was doing.

Again if we allow ourselves to join Berkeley in his hunt for the object it is only too easy to share, and when all the criticisms have been voiced, to continue to share, his dissatisfaction with the commonsense way of thinking about the matter. If we start to search for the IT which looks like this, feels like this, sounds like this, smells like this; if we begin to wonder what it can be apart from our perceptions of it, we may still remain uncomfortably puzzled.

This puzzlement may perhaps to some extent be removed by the reflection that the question we are asking may be a foolish one, that the search may be self-defeating. Are we perhaps merely asking what it would look like and feel like if no one was looking at it or touching it? And in that case the answer is obviously that it would not look or feel like anything, it would in a sense have no appearance if there was no one for it to appear to, but nevertheless we should still obstinately and commonsensibly feel that it would *really* still be there just the same. It will be useful now if we tackle the knot, and most readers will probably feel still that there *is* a knot, from a slightly different point of view by taking a look at the Concept of Reality.

THE CONCEPT OF REALITY

What do we mean by saying that something is real? It is interesting that though Philosophy has often been described and thought of as the search for ultimate reality there is surprisingly little said in philosophical literature about what it is to be real. It seems to have been for most writers a concept that was taken for granted.

It will be useful first to consider briefly how the words 'real', 'really', 'reality', are used normally, as well as by philosophers. Any findings that we make here are not likely to give us any final and conclusive answers, but they should at least be helpful.

'Real' and its relations seem to be used most often in contrast, either explicit or implicit, with what is apparent. 'It looks like an oasis but you'll find when you get closer that it's *really* just a mirage.' 'On first acquaintance he seems a thoroughly nice chap, but when you get to know him better you'll find that he's *really* rather a rogue.' 'I don't feel I've ever got to know the *real* John Smith.'

Often in our ordinary everyday experience we feel that we have found out what something *really* was as opposed to what it seemed to be: what looked like sugar turns out to be *really* salt. Sometimes we talk and think as though the reality keeps eluding us – perhaps especially when we are looking for the *real* John Smith. If we are making investigations about almost anything, John Smith's character, the causes of cancer, we may think of ourselves as stripping off successive layers of appearances in order to penetrate more closely to the hard core of reality. Even if we are successful in our search, if we find out that it's *really* salt, what *really* caused my car to stop, we would be likely to admit that what we have found is not the *ultimate* reality, but only, as it were, a *relative* reality.

Because in our experience we are continually finding that appearances are deceptive, continually enlarging our knowledge and finding out more about what things are really like, it is natural to suppose that there is an end to the search, an ultimate reality, a hard core, which will emerge when the successive layers of appearances have been stripped off.

This is a supposition that has commonly been made by philosophers. Plato distinguished the world of appearances, to which all our experiences belong and which is the object of opinion, from the unchanging world of reality, the world of the Forms or Universals, which is the object of knowledge. The contrast which we so often make in our everyday life, in what might be thought of as a trivial way, between things as they *seem*, and things as they *are*, is taken much further and deeper by philosophers in the contrast between the thing as it appears and the thing in itself, between the *phenomenal* and the *noumenal*. But whereas for our limited purposes we find out how things are, that it wasn't really a bush but just a trick played by the light, for philosophers the thing-in-itself is often by definition unknown and unknowable.

This idea of the ultimately real, the heart of the onion, recurs again and again in philosophical writings. Here are a few selections:

I hold that these unities of existence, these occasions of experience, are *the really real* things which in their collective unity compose the evolving universe, ever plunging into the creative advance. WHITEHEAD, quoted by C. E. M. Joad, *Guide to Philosophy*, p. 583.

There is not that single thing in the world, whereof we can know the real nature, or what it is in itself. . . .

their internal constitution, their true and real nature, you are utterly in the dark as to that. BERKELEY, Hylas in *Third Dialogue*, p. 262.

This life is an appearance only, that is, a sensible representation of the purely spiritual life, and the whole sensible world is a mere picture which in our present mode of knowledge hovers before us, and like a dream has in itself no objective reality; that if we could intuit ourselves and things *as they are*, we should see ourselves in a world of spiritual beings, our sole and true community which has not begun through birth, and will not cease through bodily death – both birth and death being mere appearance. KANT, quoted by E. W. F. Tomlin, *Great Philosophers of the West*, p. 213.

And Joad in representing Kant's views says:

Each of us is in direct contact with reality; but we do not perceive reality exactly as it is. C. E. M. JOAD, *Guide to Philosophy*, p. 384.

Many of those who have written about Reality in this sort of way have thought, as Plato did, of the ultimate reality of the next, the supernatural, world, whose properties will not be revealed to us, or only very dimly, in this life. And when writers are dealing with reality in these terms it is obviously important for those who read to be aware whether it is an other-worldly, by definition unknowable, reality that is being referred to, or whether an attempt is being made to deal with the Concept of Reality *in this world*, which is what we are trying to do in this chapter.

EXISTENCE

The notion of what it is to be real is of course inseparable from, and in most cases the same as, the notion of existence. Let us compare how we use the relevant words and phrases.

To ask, when we seem to see a lake in the desert, whether it is a real lake, would be the same as to ask 'Is that a lake?' To phrase the question: 'Does that lake exist?', would be an odd and unnatural thing to do, for the mere mention of 'that lake', assumes, in a sense, its existence. And this is a warning of the very important fact that if we think of existence or being real as just another property like blueness or being blue, we are likely to get into a muddle. We are, however, continually using 'real' as a contrast word in a way in which we do not use 'existence'. We might ask whether it is a real tree either because we are in doubt as to whether it is an illusion and does not really exist at all, or more probably because we want to know whether it is a dummy, made perhaps of cardboard. In the latter case there is no doubt about its existence, but some doubt about whether it is what it appears to be.

To wonder about the reality of something, therefore, may be just to wonder whether it exists; or it may be to wonder whether the view we have of it, our information about it, is merely superficial and an appearance which when stripped away will reveal something that is *more* real until eventually we get to the *really real*.

THE EMPIRICAL TEST

If we want to know whether the apparent lake is there or not we go and see whether we can get a drink out of it. For common sense the normal way and indeed the only way to testing whether an object exists is to look, and feel and listen etc. perhaps with our unassisted senses or perhaps in a more refined way with microscopes and other scientific instruments.

When we are puzzling over the theories of Berkeley, what

empirical test can we make? We have already seen the answer. Dr Johnson thought he was making one, but we have shown that on Berkeley's terms it was not acceptable; he has phrased his theory in such terms as to preclude the possibility of any empirical test. What we can do, of course, and this is what scientists are doing the whole time, is to make investigations which will enable us to see the more real by stripping off layers of appearance; the description that the scientist gives of the table on which I write is more complete and detailed than it would have been a hundred years ago, he is more fully informed about what is happening; and there is no reason to suppose that the scientist of the future will not be more fully informed still.

IS CERTAINTY ATTAINABLE?

We come now to what is perhaps the most important of all the points to be made in discussing the views of Berkeley and the general philosophical problems of Appearance and Reality. This point is summed up by Sir Isaiah Berlin thus:

Propositions are either certain and uninformative or informative and not certain. Metaphysical knowledge which claims to be both certain and informative is therefore in principle not possible. *The Age of Enlightenment*, p. 180.

We have seen that Hume strove to find certainty and failed. In his search for certainty he was compelled to keep discarding entities and ideas of which he could not feel sure, the area of certainty was continually diminished until it was reduced to the pin-point of a particular perception. He discovered that from experience and observation nothing was to be learnt with certainty.

But we do get certainty in some matters. The point that Berlin is making and the conclusion to which Hume arrived is that we can never get in the world of experience the certainty or logical necessity that we get in the closed systems of, for example, Pure Mathematics. There is nothing very remarkable about the certainty we get here, for we put it in. When we say that if A=B and B=C then A=C, we should have to qualify it by saying that it only applies to those things to which it applies: and we therefore do not allow it to be informative, it is in the last resort an analytic statement; a rose is a rose. As soon however as we start to deal with an open system, the world of experience, we can never get the complete certainty of logical necessity, though we can and do get situations in which individuals may feel a very high degree of subjective certainty. But however certain we may feel that the sun is going to set tonight it is not certain or necessary in the same way that if two quantities are each equal to a third quantity then they are equal to each other (provided that they are quantities of a kind to which the concept of precise equality can be applied).

It is easy to understand man's search for certainty through the ages and natural that because he was able to find it in some departments in the form of logical necessity he should think that it could be found too in a metaphysical system which would give an account of the fundamentals of experience based on a similarly solid rock and not on the shifting sands of appearance.

To quote Berlin again:

This craving for a metaphysical system is one of the most obsessive of all the fantasies which has dominated human minds. *The Age of Enlightenment*, p. 190.

There seems to be no doubt that a fantasy is what it is and that the writings of Hume have contributed considerably to the demonstration that this is so.

SUMMARY

(1) There is much to be learnt from the study of Berkeley's writings and if we try to understand fully the nature of the problem with which he was wrestling we see that his theory was much less absurd than is often supposed.

(2) But unless a theory such as his is logically self-contradictory it cannot be proved or refuted with certainty. It is a theory about the world around us concerning which we can only learn by experience and observation. Such experience can never give us certainty. There is the additional point that Berkeley phrased his theory in such a way as to make an empirical refutation impossible.

(3) On the whole the most sensible and useful way to describe our experiences for everyday non-scientific purposes would seem to be to say that material objects exist out there and that we see them, feel them, hear them etc. But it is important to realize that this is merely a convenient way to group our experiences. Scientists are increasingly finding that for their purposes, in order to increase their ability to predict and control, it is convenient to group them differently.

The culmination of 300 years of the ostensible study of material bodies has been the production of the equations of the electromagnetic field, the field equations of relativity, the wave equation of the electron, and the laws of thermodynamics. Where in that magnificent epitome of knowledge does one find the least indication that it is a world of material objects that is being described? H. DINGLE, *The Scientific Adventure*, p. 203.

In other words, as a result of studying what were first thought of as material bodies, scientists are coming more and more to the conclusion that the material object is not a useful postulate.

(4) In speculating about objects and about reality we must be careful not to make inquiries which are phrased in such a way as to make answers impossible. Questions which are equivalent to: 'What does that look like when no one is looking at it?' or 'What is an object like in itself apart from our sensations, perceptions, experience of it?' are surely foolish because in principle unanswerable. We may arrive at views about the world of experience which are more and more real by devising and using better and better instruments. And scientists may, by grouping experiences differently, arrive at conclusions which are more and more useful. But there is no final conclusion. When we have removed all the layers of experience there really *is* nothing there – and in this respect the analogy of the onion is rather a good one, except that we must not think of the layers as being discarded and thrown away. (Perhaps the *real* reason why peeling an onion brings tears to the eyes is because it epitomizes the inevitable failure of the search for the hard core of reality!)

If the reader remains puzzled about the search for I T, the hard core of reality, let him remember that the hunt really is a bogus one. What is being asked is what is I T like apart from all the things that we know about it and possibly can know about it; any discovery that is made cannot qualify to *be* I T, it is inevitably *about* I T. As so often the possibility of an answer is seen to be put out of court by the nature of the question.

Exercises

1. Do you find, with Locke, that you are able to form the abstract idea of redness apart from particular red objects, or do you agree with Berkeley that it is impossible?

2. It has been suggested that a reason why cows are such timorous animals is that their eyes are so constituted that they see human beings and other animals much larger than they really are.

   Does this seem to you to be likely?

3. How would you check the claim of a man who has been blind from birth that he knows what pink looks like?

4. Most people would say that tables continue to exist when not perceived but that toothaches and feelings of envy do not.

   Discuss why this should be so. Do you agree?

5. ... for we are not unfrequently deceived in the same manner when awake; as when persons in the jaundice see all objects yellow, or when the stars or bodies at a great distance appear to us much smaller than they are. DESCARTES, *A Discourse on Method*, p. 32.

   How near should we have to be to the stars in order that they should appear the right size?

6. In Berkeley's *First Dialogue* Philonous tries to persuade Hylas that the various qualities of objects perceived by the senses cannot exist without the mind.

The following is an extract:

PHILONOUS: What! Are then the beautiful red and purple we see on yonder clouds, really in them? Or do you imagine they have in themselves any other form than that of a dark mist or vapour?

HYLAS: I must own, Philonous, those colours are not really in the clouds as they seem to be at this distance. They are only apparent colours.

PHILONOUS: *Apparent* call you them? how shall we distinguish these apparent colours from real?

HYLAS: Very easily. Those are to be thought apparent, which, appearing only at a distance, vanish upon a nearer approach.

BERKELEY, p. 214.

How would you continue the argument if you were Philonous?

7. All things exist as they are perceived: at least in relation to the percipient. 'The mind is its own place, and of itself can make a Heaven of Hell, a Hell of Heaven.' But poetry defeats the curse which binds us to be subjected to the accident of surrounding impressions. P. B. SHELLEY, 'A Defence of Poetry'. *Prose Works*, ed. H. Buxton Forman, Vol. 3, p. 139.

Do the first two sentences seem to you to be making the same or different points? And how does the third fit in?

8. '... it becomes plain that the existence of a table in space is related to my experience of *it* in precisely the same way as the existence of my own experience is related to my experience of *that*. Of both we are merely aware: if we are aware that the one exists, we are aware in precisely the same sense that the other exists; and if it is true that my experience can exist, even when I do not happen to be aware of its existence, we have exactly the same reason for supposing that the table can do so also. When, therefore, Berkeley supposed that the only thing

of which I am directly aware is my own sensations and ideas, he supposed what was false ... I am as directly aware of the existence of material things in space as of my own sensations; and *what* I am aware of with regard to each is exactly the same – namely that in one case the material thing and in the other case my sensation does really exist. G. E. MOORE 'The Refutation of Idealism', in *Philosophical Studies*, pp. 29, 30.

Discuss, with particular reference to the 'relationships' in the first sentence. Do you feel that you are as directly aware of the existence of material things as of your own sensations?

Supplementary passages

Some quotations illustrating the ways in which Appearance and Reality have been thought about.

(1) '... and yet there *is* a sense in which the painter creates a bed, isn't there?'

'Yes,' he agreed, 'he produces an appearance of one.'

'And what about the carpenter? Didn't you agree that what he produces is not the essential Form of Bed, the ultimate reality, but a particular bed?'

'I did.'

'If so, then what he makes is not the ultimate reality, but something that resembles that reality. And anyone who says that the products of the carpenter or any other craftsman are ultimate realities can hardly be telling the truth, can he?'

'No one familiar with the sort of arguments we're using could suppose so.'

'So we shan't be surprised if the bed the carpenter makes lacks the precision of reality?'

'No.'

'Then shall we try to define representation now, in the light of this illustration?'

'Yes, please.'

'We have seen that there are three sorts of bed. The first exists in the ultimate nature of things, and if it was made by anyone it must, I suppose, have been made by God. The second is made by the carpenter, the third by the painter.'

'Yes, that is so.'

'So painter, carpenter, and God are each responsible for one kind of bed.'

'Yes.'

'God created only one essential Form of Bed in the ultimate nature of things, either because he wanted to or because some necessity prevented him from making more than one; at any rate he didn't produce more than one, and more than one could not possibly be produced.'

'Why?'

'Because, suppose he created two only, you would find that they both shared a common character or form, and this common character would be the ultimate reality.'

'That's true.'

'And I suppose that God knew it, and as he wanted to be the real creator of a real Bed, and not just a carpenter making a particular bed, decided to make the ultimate reality unique.' ...
'But tell me, which does the painter try to represent? The ultimate reality or the things the craftsman makes?'

'The things the craftsman makes?'

'As they are, or as they appear? There is still that distinction to make.'

'I don't understand', he said.

'What I mean is this. If you look at a bed, or anything else, sideways, or endways or from some other angle, does it make any difference to the bed? Isn't it merely that it looks different?'

'Yes, it's the same bed, but it looks different.'

'Then consider – does the painter try to represent the bed or other object as it is, or as it appears? Does he represent it as it is, or as it looks?'

'As it looks.' PLATO, *The Republic*, trans. by H. D. P. Lee, pp. 372–4.

(2) It is mere superstition to suppose that an appeal to experience can prove *reality*. That I find something in existence in the world or in myself, shows that this something *exists*, and it cannot show *more*. Any deliverance of consciousness – whether original or acquired – is but a deliverance of consciousness. It is in no case an oracle and a revelation which we have to accept. It is a fact, like other facts, to be dealt with; and there is no presumption anywhere that any *fact* is better than appearance. F. H. BRADLEY, *Appearance and Reality*, p. 206.

(3) He who installs himself in becoming sees in duration the very life of things, the fundamental reality. HENRI BERGSON, *Creative Evolution*, p. 335.

(4) The following passage from the Reith Lectures of 1950 by a distinguished biologist, J. Z. Young, shows again the modern scientific view of the relativity of the world we seem to know:

By the use of the new exact ways of measuring time and distance the scientists [of the seventeenth century] built up a picture of a distinct world, the 'real' or 'material' world, as it came to be called, outside man. . . . This is the world that we are apt to feel so sure 'exists' around us today. . . . What I am going to say is that the form we give to this world is a construct of our brains, using such observations as they have been able to make. . . .

In some sense we literally create the world we speak about . . . we cannot speak simply as if there is a world around us of which our senses give true information. In trying to speak about what the world is like we must remember all the time that what we see and what we say depends on what we have learned; we ourselves come into the process. J. Z. YOUNG, *Doubt and Certainty in Science*, pp. 107–8.

FREE WILL AND DETERMINISM

CAUSATION

IT seems reasonable to suppose that ever since men have existed they have made investigations into the world in which they found themselves. As we have already remarked the gain in knowledge, especially in the last fifty years, has been immense. This gain has been due to the efforts of scientists who have meticulously and methodically noted facts and events, and have sought for connexions between them. For our knowledge to be useful it must be orderly. It can only become orderly when we notice that there is an order about the events which we observe, that things seem to happen according to certain principles, that there is a uniformity in what we find in nature. We discover that certain events seem always to occur together and in a certain sequence; that if I knock my pen on the table on which I am writing I hear a noise of a certain kind; that if I take my glasses off I can't see what I have written; that if I put my foot against a chair and push, the chair will move. We say that certain events 'cause' certain other events, and though the precise nature of this causal link is philosophically puzzling, no particular difficulties arise for the ordinary man or for the scientist if he takes it for granted. The scientist is concerned to discover and analyse in greater detail more links in causal chains; the botanist finds that the burying of a particular seed is followed some time later by the emergence in the same place of a certain plant – he thinks that the one event *causes* the other, but he wants to know *how*. He wants to know what happens in between; he wants to fill in as much detail as possible in the chain of cause and effect. The scientist is also obviously concerned in investigating new chains of cause and effect; the chemist wants to discover what will happen if he mixes this with that; a board of inquiry is set up to find out why the aeroplane crashed. We may be looking for the effects of a certain set of causes, for the causes of certain effects, or for intermediate causes and effects between a known cause and a known effect. In every case what we normally take for granted is that events are linked in this way, that a certain set of causes will always be followed by the same effect. If we were to find a case where this seemed not to be true, where the same set of causes was followed by a different effect, our reaction would certainly be to suppose that the set of causes could not after all have been the same, rather than to suppose that our assumption about the uniformity of nature, about the same causes producing the same effect, was wrong.

Scientists have been making investigations of this kind into the principles that govern the interactions of inanimate objects with increasing success, and their success is measured by the extent to which they are enabled to *predict* what is going to happen in the future, and also even more importantly, to *control* it – to prevent certain undesirable events, to bring about desirable ones. It would probably be generally agreed that the inanimate universe is in principle mechanistic, that all events in it are mechanically caused, and that scientists will continue to find out more about the ways in which these causes operate.

Not only have mechanical chains of cause and effect been investigated with increasing success, but also psychological ones. The comparatively new science of psychology aims to explain and in some cases also to predict, human behaviour. The ways in which we think and act and also the workings of the human brain are scrutinized by scientists.

It is worth noticing that the causes of human behaviour are of two kinds – there is first of all what is usually described as a *mechanical* or *efficient* cause ('I was late because I had hurt my leg and couldn't walk any faster'); and there is also what is called a *final* cause in terms of motive or purpose ('I was late in order to avoid the first half hour of what I thought would be a very boring party'). It is true that in a very close analysis this distinction may be difficult to uphold, but nevertheless it is broadly useful. For many, perhaps most, human actions causes of both these kinds are operating in conjunction.

Scientists also try to discover what physical, mechanical, events in the brain are accompanying or 'causing' the actions which the individual performs, the decisions which he makes. It is no part of our present purpose to get involved in the very difficult problem of the relationship between mind and body, or to discuss whether it is sensible to suppose that the concept of mind as ordinarily thought of is a useful one. The point we are concerned to make here is that psychologists and other scientists are much occupied in modern times with the attempt to explain human behaviour. It is often the case that the kind of human behaviour in which they are most interested is behaviour that is odd, eccentric, anti-social. Explanation of the behaviour will sometimes be in terms of the subconscious which, it may be claimed, has been affected by events in the early history of the individual, perhaps even when he was still in the womb. Psychologists will often be trying to explain the behaviour because they feel that if they can find the causes they can take suitable remedial action and get the patient to behave differently. What they are interested in is controlling and curing, and to this end the study of psychological chains of cause and effect and the prediction which follows from it is obviously of great importance. Psychologists would be the first to admit, however, that they are much less able to predict human behaviour than other scientists are to predict events in the world of physical objects. They might also say that this is at least in part because they know less about it – their science is a comparatively new one. But they would be likely to claim that their investigations are being increasingly successful. This increasing success seems to lead more and more to the conclusion that all behaviour can be explained in terms of the individual's past history and present circumstances and disposition.

THE DETERMINIST VIEW

From such considerations of what seems to be the fact that psychological events too are subject to the laws of cause and effect, it is natural that an entirely mechanistic or determinist view of the universe should be suggested. If every event has a cause or set of causes, and if the same set of causes always and inevitably produces the same result, it would seem to be the logical conclusion that once the world was set in train what happened was inevitable, could not have been otherwise, was determined from the beginning.

Many people might accept this as far as the 'merely mechanical' events are concerned. They would be likely to agree that before there was life in the universe the movements of the planets were subject to merely mechanical laws, and that their position and motion at any time were completely determined by their position and motion at any previous time. People on the whole, however, are very reluctant indeed to accept the view that their own actions are 'determined' in the same way as the movements of the planets; this view conflicts with the very strongly held conviction that we all have that our wills are *free*.

THE DILEMMA STATED

We propose now to have a look at the apparent dilemma posed by the question: 'Are our wills free, or are our actions determined? We shall find on investigation that there is in fact much less of a dilemma than appears at first sight, that when we examine closely the two alternatives and the language in which they are expressed, the difficulties to some considerable extent fade away.

Let us briefly take a closer look at the two apparently incompatible positions.

There is no doubt at all that in most of our thinking we assume that people will behave in what we should describe as a rational way in the situations in which they find themselves. We assume, that is to say, that their actions will be explicable in terms of the circumstances or context in which they are performed, and in terms of the character or nature of the actors and the purposes which they have in mind. Their actions we should certainly say are determined by *them*, but their characters, their purposes, their circumstances, are the product of their heredity, their education, their environment, the whole of their past history. They act as they do because they are what they are, and they are what they are because of events in the past, including their own actions, which have made them what they are. What they do, in other words, is caused or determined by the total situation including their own nature or character, in which their actions are performed. Every action therefore seems to be at least in principle predictable. It could not be other than it is. It follows inevitably from all that has gone before.

'On the other hand', a believer in free will might retort, 'I am convinced by the most direct and immediate evidence possible, the evidence of my own experience and feeling, that my will is free, that my actions are not predetermined, that I can do what I like. Look, I decide to raise my right arm – now my left. Here I am *exercising* my free will, *demonstrating* that the choice is mine and mine only.' It has also been argued that not only is the theory of determinism contrary to facts of experience of this kind, but that also it makes nonsense of any notion of human responsibility, that it leaves no place for ethics, for good and evil; even that it makes truth impossible, that if determinism is true, there is no such thing as truth. (See passage from H. W. B. Joseph on pages 225–6.) The whole point of moral praise and blame, it is argued, is that man freely chooses between what is right and what is wrong, that he could have acted otherwise. If all his actions are determined, if free will is an illusion, and he really has no choice, then praise and blame are futile and meaningless. (It might also be noted that they are inevitable; people *do* praise and blame, and if these actions are determined there is no point in saying they are meaningless any more than there is any point in saying that there is no point in saying that they are meaningless: and so on in an infinite and inevitable regress.)

THE DILEMMA EXAMINED

This dilemma has been in the past, though not so much in the comparatively recent past, a source of much controversy and puzzlement. In its present situation it seems fair to say that the problem is a typically philosophical one, in the sense that any solution or any claim to a solution is likely to be attained by speculation or thought, rather than by investigation. We know that certain happenings cause and are caused by certain other happenings, and we know that this is true, not only of events in the merely physical world, but also of events in which human beings are concerned in which they make decisions and act. It would seem to be almost impossible not to accept the fact that people act as they do for certain reasons – that their actions are caused. There is clearly much more that we might eventually find out and would greatly like to find out, about the details and principles of psychological causation, and perhaps too about the nature of the causal link in general, but it seems doubtful whether any further knowledge of this kind that we could gain would throw any more light on the problem with which we are now wrestling – the problem of free will and determinism. We know pretty well what the facts are – the question is how to describe them. No further evidence from the psychologists or the scientist is going to be of much assistance to us.

If we accept that there is a problem or dilemma it looks as though the knot must be of our own making. There seem to be two accounts of the matter, both of which we know in a sense to be perfectly true. These accounts do not at first sight seem to agree with each other and the problem is how to reconcile them. In order to do this an essential step is to examine and analyse carefully the language in which the accounts are couched. The key words in the dilemma as it has been posed are obviously 'free' and 'determined'. Let us take a look at them.

When we use the word 'free' we normally imply free from something, or free for something. And when we claim that our wills are free we mean that our choices are not determined by forces from outside, that we are free from external compulsions, that our decisions are made by ourselves. We certainly do not want to say that our actions are uncaused. People are normally very ready to give reasons for what they do, though they may sometimes stress the fact that the reason just was their choice ('I just thought I would'; 'It was the whim of the moment'), and the point of talking about *free* will is usually to emphasize that actions *are* determined by those who perform them.

But what do we mean by 'determined'? This word requires careful examination. In some contexts it can be replaced by 'caused' without much change of meaning ('what happened was determined – caused – by the events that preceded it'), though in using it rather than 'caused' we probably want to suggest the inevitability of what happened, the fact that it could not have been otherwise. There are other contexts however in which 'determined' can very definitely not be replaced by 'caused'. If I say, 'What will happen tomorrow is now determined', the word 'caused' as ordinarily used would not perform the same job. The implication would seem to be that what will happen is in some sense now decided, is at least in principle predictable and perhaps in fact predictable. It is not difficult to see how the fact that 'determined' may be used with these different meanings can lead to a dilemma or bewitchment. To say that events in the future will be caused by other events is not necessarily at all the same thing as to say that they are now decided and can be predicted. We are likely to think more clearly about the matter if we try to avoid 'determined' and use instead either 'caused', 'decided' or 'predictable'.

PREDICTABILITY

From the premisses that all events are caused and that the
same set of causes must always produce the same effects it
seems natural to infer that if we can become acquainted with
all the causes it should be at least in principle possible to
predict with certainty what is going to happen. This idea,
though attractive at first sight, contains a basic fallacy which
is largely responsible for the free will – determinism
muddle. In order to examine this, at the risk of some
repetition of what has been said in earlier chapters, we must
take another look at the contrast between what is *necessary*
and what is *contingent*, and at the concept of certainty.

If A, B and C are three positive numbers and if A is
greater than B, and B is greater than C, then we can say that
it follows necessarily that A is greater than C. Once we have
understood the idea of number and what is meant by
'greater than' we can see that it is inconceivable that it
should be otherwise. No event happening in the real world
can prevent this being true; it is true of necessity. But it
should be noticed that we make it true by putting the
necessity in, by our definitions of the terms we use, by
constructing the closed system of pure mathematics and
insulating it from the events of the real world.

Suppose, however, that A, B and C are three tennis
players, that A always beats B very easily, and B always
beats C very easily. Can we say that it follows necessarily
that A will beat C? Obviously not. All sorts of other events
might intervene. A might slip and break his ankle, or have a
fit. C might just have been pretending to be a bad player.
What in fact will happen is said to be 'contingent'; that is to
say, conditional, dependent on other things. We might say

that it will follow necessarily that A will beat C provided that they both play according to their normal form, and that there are no accidents. But we can only claim necessity here by putting it in, by saying that it will happen if nothing occurs to stop it, which amounts in effect to saying that it will happen if it happens. Nothing in the real world of contingent events happens of necessity.

In their ordinary thinking, people on the whole accept this. However certain they may feel that something will happen they will be prepared to admit that it *may* be prevented by some unforeseen event, an earthquake or other natural calamity. But they are inclined to feel that this lack of certainty is due merely to lack of knowledge and that if we knew the whole situation, all the causes, we should be able to predict the future with certainty. Although they might be prepared to admit that in fact we never shall know the whole situation, it might still be thought that the future is *in principle* completely predictable, in a sense therefore decided.

The answer to this – and it is a very important answer – is that the total situation, the number of potential causes, is indefinitely large, and is not therefore even in principle completely knowable. Not only is it obviously impossible for any human mind to be fully informed about all events and happenings in the Universe, but it is impossible also in principle for everything to be known about an unlimited Universe. However much is known, there is always something else. Although therefore it is perfectly possible to say that all events are caused, in no sense is it possible to say that what will happen tomorrow is now definitely decided, is in principle completely predictable.

The realization of this fact need not stop us and should not stop us from continuing to do all we can to predict the future with increasing confidence. As we have already pointed out, scientists of every kind, including psychologists, have been engaged for many years with considerable success in increasing the scope and accuracy of their predictions. The fact that their success can never be complete should not discourage them. It is a common fallacy of human thinking to suppose that every metaphorical mountain must have a peak; that because there are better ways of doing things, there must always be a perfect way; that because some objects give more aesthetic pleasure than others there must be an ultimate goal of absolute beauty or beauty in itself. It may be helpful to anyone who is tempted to think on these lines, to ask himself in what time the 'perfect' mile would be run. The fact that everyone realizes that not only is it a physical impossibility but also a logical impossibility for the mile to be run in no time at all, does not prevent mankind from continually trying to improve the record. Similarly the fact that complete predictability is a logical impossibility should not prevent mankind from continuing to predict.

CERTAINTY

It will be useful here to say a few words about the concept of certainty. The adjective 'certain' is probably most often used to describe a state of mind. We all know what it is to feel certain about something, but most of us have had the experience of feeling certain, saying that we were certain, and then being proved to be wrong. It might be argued in such a case that we could not have been certain after all. Such an argument would inevitably revolve round the way in which the word 'certain' is to be used; if it is to be applied merely to a state of mind then the evidence of the owner of the state must surely be decisive as to whether he is (feels) certain or not, though it is relevant to note the point that some people are much more easily persuaded to be certain about things than others. Most people would probably agree under cross-examination that usually when they say 'certain' they really mean 'almost certain', and that as we have just been arguing, it is not rational to feel completely certain about contingent events in the real world.

The adjective 'certain' however is used not only to describe states of mind but also in such phrases as 'it is certain that . . .' to imply what might be described as an objective certainty. I suggest that when the word is used like this what is usually meant is either that the speaker or writer is certain himself and is perhaps claiming also that a great many other people are too, or that it is logically necessary. It does not seem reasonable to hold that there is any sense in which there can be certainty 'in the events'.

It may well be, however, that the fact that the word 'certainty' is sometimes used to describe a psychological state and sometimes to describe a logical necessity, has been responsible for some confusion of thought. The aspect of determinism that people find particularly unpalatable is the idea that what they are going to do is determined, in the sense of decided; that is must certainly happen. We can see now, however, that this is at least misleading. For if by 'certainly' happening is meant 'necessarily' happening this is not true, for in the contingent world nothing happens of necessity, and if the 'certainly' merely implies that some people feel sure, we know very well how easily they may be wrong.

'FREE' WILL FROM DIFFERENT POINTS OF VIEW

Further illumination of the problem and loosening of the knot may be obtained by a consideration of the possible different points of view. There is the point of view first of the individual exercising his free will, secondly of another individual watching him doing so, and thirdly of an imaginary individual observing from right outside the system of cause and effect.

As we have already seen, the individual, considering his own actions, is firmly convinced that in the ordinary sense of the word his will is free. He can do what he wishes – whatever he does he could have acted differently. What he does could not have been determined yesterday because he had not then decided what he was going to do. He is making up his mind as he goes along.

Another individual, however, or set of individuals, watching his actions will use somewhat different language about it. It is probably true today that a greater proportion of the population than ever before – psychologists, economists, social scientists, advertising agents – is engaged in attempting to predict how people will behave in certain situations. They assume that the behaviour that they are investigating is a function of the man behaving and the situation in which he finds himself. They find that what people do can be predicted with varying degrees of confidence, though they would be the first to admit that prediction is a very difficult business and that all the answers will never be known.

The situation is further complicated by the fact that the act of prediction is likely to affect and alter that which is being predicted. This is analogous to Heisenberg's famous uncertainty principles which states that the act of measuring involves a transfer of energy between what is measuring and what is being measured, and therefore alters both, so that in principle there can be no such things as completely objective measurement.

The act of prediction may make what is being predicted either more or less likely to happen. If the city editor of a Sunday paper predicts that the price of shares in a certain company will go up next week, it is almost certain that they will go up, for investors will rush to buy them in the hope and expectation of making a profit, and this increased demand will send the price up. The act of prediction here causes what is predicted to happen.

If, however, it is predicted in a newspaper that there will be an unprecedented traffic jam at a certain place at a certain time, the act of prediction is likely to prevent that happening, since motorists will tend to avoid it. It is easy to think of many other examples of the same principle at work.

The point about the imaginary observer whom we supposed to be right outside the machine is, of course, that the happenings which we are considering would be insulated from any possible effect of his predictions. Such an observer would surely judge that the actions of people are caused by their nature, the whole of their past history and their past decisions, and the complex of events in which they find themselves, and he might be imagined as predicting with greater success than if he were involved in the machine. But, as we have already suggested, since the number of variables to be considered is potentially indefinitely large, it seems at least doubtful whether it makes sense to say that actions are even 'in principle' completely and infallibly predictable.

'COULD HAVE...'

A main point that anyone who is arguing in favour of free will is likely to make is that in any situation, whatever he does in fact do, he 'could have' acted differently. And it would also be argued that unless it is assumed that people 'could have' done otherwise, there is no meaning in moral praise or blame. 'You ought to have done so and so', must surely imply that you *could have* done it. We will now examine this phrase and try to analyse it.

In order to perform a conscious deliberate action the individual must have the ability (physical or mental) and the opportunity; and he must also choose to do it. For Jones to lift a weight of 200 lbs he must be strong enough to lift it, the weight must be there for him to lift, and he must make a decision or choose to lift it. It is interesting that the phrase 'I can' is used either about ability without opportunity ('I can type at twenty words a minute' – though in fact there is no typewriter here), or about ability and opportunity combined ('I can see you for ten minutes now' – though after that there are a lot of other appointments). Sometimes, as in the last example, the emphasis is on opportunity, but in such a case the ability is assumed, and we should never say 'I can' if the opportunity is present but the ability lacking. (Though we might of course say, 'I could if...') The 'I can' does not cover choice, and indeed is often used to emphasize that the choice is lacking. ('I can, but I won't.')

The next point to make is the grammatical one that the 'could' of 'I could have' may be either 'was able to' or 'would have been able to'. In the latter case there must obviously be an 'if' clause, either expressed or understood. Sometimes this will indicate that either the ability or the opportunity was lacking ('I could have run that mile in ten minutes if I hadn't twisted my ankle'; 'I could have said a few rather effective words if anyone had asked me'). But there is no problem or difficulty about such cases and it is not relevant to our present purpose to consider them. We are interested in the cases where it is claimed that the ability and opportunity were present, but the choice was lacking, as when someone says, 'I could (was able to) have done so and so, but didn't.' The question we obviously have to ask is in what sense, if any, he *could* have chosen differently. Ability-to-choose must now be examined.

It is worth noticing that the claim that a person could have chosen differently can never be verified or falsified, though claims about ability or opportunity may be. No subsequent action that you perform or act of choice that you make can demonstrate satisfactorily your claim that you were able to have chosen other than you did on a particular past occasion. The question, 'Could he have chosen otherwise?' is in a sense unanswerable and obviously therefore a not very satisfactory question.

A man chooses in accordance with what he wants or likes, but at least in the short run we do not seem able to like differently, to alter our scale of preferences. If I have always preferred ice cream to tapioca pudding, it is not possible for me suddenly to change this preference. Perhaps I can in the long run, but only if there is some reason for me to do so: to please someone I am fond of, or just as a bit of psychological investigation to show that it is possible, or because I feel I am missing something – everyone else seems to get so much pleasure out of tapioca pudding that I really must cultivate my palate and give it another try.

I act then according to my choice; my choice is in accordance with (caused by) my motives, my plans, my scale of preferences, and this 'I' that chooses is a complex evolving personality that is changing and developing the whole time. So far, we have as it were taken the 'I' for granted. There is a tendency to think of the 'I' that chooses as an entity that is apart from, in some senses above, the desires, the hopes and fears and reasonings which provide the evidence or the material for the choice. Professor Ryle has called this tendency the myth of the 'ghost in the machine'. The great danger and mistake in thinking about it like this is that this entity tends to be thought about as something that is separate and unchanging.

It would seem, however, that a much more realistic way to think about it is that what I do at any moment is caused by the whole of my complex personality at that moment, but the decision I make, what I do, subtly alters this personality. If we reflect, it is surely obvious that, in a very important sense, what we are is changing the whole time. Our knowledge, our experience, our purposes, our desires, our preferences, are altering and evolving and, in a sense, all that I am and the whole of my past, has produced or caused me-deciding or me-choosing at this moment. When I say 'I could have acted differently' the 'I', standing for the whole of the personality at that moment, includes the decision to act as I did. For the past to have been different, either the situation must have been different (and we are implicitly assuming it to have been the same), or the 'I' that chose, decided, must have been different. For me to have acted differently in the same situation I would have had to have *been* different.

We can say therefore that in the sense in which we are using the terms, 'I was able to do have done something other than what I did' cannot be true. But this is obviously not a psychological discovery. It follows with logical necessity from the definition of the terms. It is suggested, however, that a careless use of these terms, a failure to think out what it is sensible to mean by them, may have resulted in much muddled use of the sentence, 'I could have done otherwise.'

It may be argued that if there is this sense in which 'I could not have done otherwise' is true of the past, similar propositions are true of the present and the future. It is of course the case that I can only do what I will do in the sense that for me to do other than what I do is a logical impossibility. But what I will do is as yet undetermined, it is going to be decided by me, choosing freely (that is without external restraint). Anyone who is well acquainted with the situation and with my personality may succeed in predicting what I will do, but he may be wrong. What I did in the past is specific and is obviously now decided. What I will do in the future is not decided, and will depend on me (even if I say I have made up my mind, some other event may well intervene to prevent me or to make me alter my choice).

PRAISE AND BLAME

We consider now the question of moral praise and blame, and the suggestion that has been made that if a man 'could not have acted otherwise' they become inappropriate and indeed meaningless.

It is worth noticing that praise and blame are not in all their uses a proper pair of alternatives. We may praise the creator or his creation, but though we praise a book that entertains or instructs us we do not use the word 'blame' to describe our attitude to one that fails to do these things. In the case of a book the creation can be considered apart from the creator; if however we are praising an innings at cricket, or the singing of a song, we inevitably praise the agent as well as, perhaps rather than, the action. We are praising the person and his skill together, usually because of the pleasure they give us, and we may take no thought about how that skill has been acquired, about any notion of responsibility. But if we learn that the cricketer was struggling against some physical handicap, that the singer only acquired his skill as a result of many years of arduous training, we may praise too their courage or their determination. We praise them then because they refrained from acting otherwise. The cricketer did not retire because he was in pain, the singer persisted when he must have felt tired and discouraged. Notice that we should never say that we 'blamed' the innings or the song, and if we blamed the batsman or the singer it would be less likely to be for a lack of skill (unless we felt they had failed to acquire it because of some moral defect) than for a careless mistake, or for not trying as hard as they might. It seems to be the case that we distribute blame only when we think that responsibility is involved, that they could and should have done otherwise, but we praise people for the possession of skills for which they are not normally thought of as being responsible. It is interesting that many people, especially the young, would much prefer to be thought clever and rather idle, than comparatively stupid and exceedingly industrious, though it would be generally agreed that it is much more within our power to become industrious than it is to become clever. People, in other words, often prefer to be praised for a natural gift for which they are not responsible, than for an acquired characteristic for which they are. (It is of course very reasonable to prefer to *be* clever and idle, since one can perhaps become industrious. It is less reasonable to be *proud* of one's intelligence and slightly ashamed of one's industry.)

But although praise and blame are not a proper pair in their general use they are more or less so in the particular use in which we are now interested – their use as applied to people in their moral behaviour.

The suggestion we have to consider is that if a man could not have done otherwise, he can hardly be blamed for doing what he did. We have seen that the sense in which 'I could not have done otherwise' is true is that the individual, being what he was at that moment, including the decision he was making, chose that, and if he had chosen differently he would have *been* different. Clearly if there is to be any blame it must be on the individual for being what he was rather than for doing what he did. It might then be suggested that the individual couldn't help being what he was, that the state of his personality at that moment was caused by the complex of external situations through which he had passed and the decisions he had made, the things that he had done, each of which at the moment of doing them, he could not have done otherwise. There seems to be a sense therefore in which he could not have *been* otherwise.

The essential point of course about this objection is that it is being suggested that the agent was not *responsible* for his actions. From the premiss 'X could not have acted otherwise' it is inferred 'therefore X was not responsible for what he did'.

It should by now be clear that this argument, as it is usually applied, is fallacious. If it was meant that X could not have acted otherwise because of some external physical compulsion, if Maud failed to go into the garden because an irate father had locked her in her room, then it would clearly be true to say that there was no responsibility. But if it is meant that X could not have acted otherwise because of what he was, then this is merely another way of saying that X *was* responsible, he acted as he did because he was what he was, it was precisely his character, the fact that he was X and no one else, that caused, was responsible for, his action.

This notion of responsibility is perhaps easier to understand if we look forward into the future rather than backward into the past. I think that I am responsible for the actions that I will perform and to some considerable extent for the sort of person that I will become, I think that I can modify my character by behaving in a certain way, for example by regularly getting up an hour earlier. I haven't quite decided yet whether I will or not. The fact that this idea came from a suggestion that someone else made or from a book that I read, or that it is designed to fulfil some purpose, makes it no less true that *I* will make the decision and that my action will modify my character and will perhaps make a difference to my future behaviour. Nor is my responsibility diminished by the fact that even though I say that I have not yet decided what I will do, others who know me well may predict accurately my behaviour in this respect.

Just as it is easier and more useful to think of responsibility with reference to the future, so too with praise and blame. We praise a man for his moral actions because we think that what he has done was to the benefit of the community (or according to God's Will or whatever our criterion for right action may be); we praise him for what he was, although obviously we do not for a moment suppose that our praise can make any difference to what he was. We certainly do suppose however that our praise may make a difference to what he, and other people too who are aware of the praise, may become in the future. Praise and blame, attitudes of approval and condemnation, are likely to make a difference to the way in which people behave. We all know very well from our personal experience that our decisions are affected by praise and blame in the past and anticipated praise and blame in the future. They form part of the complex of causes which will affect the future, but since these causes are indefinitely numerous the future is not decided yet and not completely predictable. Praising and blaming also, like any other action, are caused by the past, by the performances of the people to whom they are directed, and the characters of those who are approving or condemning.

It is suggested then that praise and blame should be thought of primarily as instruments which actually do, when given, modify the behaviour of those to whom they are directed, and, perhaps even more important, the anticipation of which is also likely to modify behaviour.

It is worth noticing that praise and blame form part of the armoury of rewards and punishments. Modern thinking about punishment tends to stress the desirability of its deterrent effect and its reformative effect, and many people regard it as immoral that there should be any retributive element. In other words punishment is thought of as an instrument for modifying future behaviour and the motive of punishing for revenge is thought of as likely to have undesirable effects on him who punishes.

It is also often pointed out that punishment merely as retribution serves no useful purpose; it is to the future we should be looking, not to the past. (In practice, of course, it is very difficult to separate these elements. A punishment given frankly for revenge, to get one's own back, may well have a considerable deterrent effect.) Similarly it might be argued that blame too should be forward looking. If someone says 'You can't blame him, he couldn't help it' we can agree that in a sense, as we have seen he couldn't, but we can go on to say that by blaming him, expressing our disapproval, we may assist him to 'help it', to avoid such action in the future. (It is of course also true that in some cases, if the individual is particularly contra-suggestible, our disapproval may make a repetition of the offence more and not less likely.)

Although blame may be more useful if it looks to the future, the fact remains that a great deal of the blaming that goes on is, like the retributive element in punishment, directed only to the past. When people are being blamed for their delinquencies, however, it is increasingly realized that for some people the choice is harder than for others. We blame people because of their immoral or anti-social behaviour. We blame them for being what they are or for what they were when they did it. But if we discover that they have never had explained to them why the action was anti-social, or what it was to be anti-social, that they have lived in an environment where actions of this kind have been approved, we would be inclined to blame them less. We blame them less because they have been insufficiently blamed in the past. It would have been very surprising if under those circumstances they had done the right thing. Their misdemeanour was easily predictable.

But although this increasing tendency to make allowances for various forms of delinquency on the grounds that 'They knew no better', 'They never had a chance', is clearly perfectly reasonable up to a point, there is a danger that it will diminish too much the extent to which a person is held responsible for his actions. This notion of responsibility, that we are capable of choosing and that we shall be approved if we choose in one way and blamed if we choose in another, is certainly, as most people know very well from

their personal experience, a strong element in the complex
of causes which affect our decisions.

SUMMARY

To say that the conclusion is that our wills are free, that our
actions are caused by us, might give rise to the comment,
'This is where we came in.' It is inevitable that in discussing
a philosophical puzzle of this kind we may be left with the
feeling that we came out 'by that same door where in we
went'. Nevertheless it is to be hoped that the reader may
feel that if there has been for him a knot of bewilderment in
this matter the knot has been to some extent loosened by
the arguments we have considered.

These may be summed up as follows:

Although from a given set of causes the same result must
always follow there is no logical necessity about events in
the world around us, and the future is not even in principle
completely predictable. This is because the number of
potential causes is indefinitely large, and also because
the attempt to predict may affect that which is being
predicted.

The general puzzlement about the problem seems to
arise partly from a confusion between what is necessary and
what is contingent, the application of the rigidities of a
closed system to the uncertainties of an open one, partly
from ambiguities in the words 'determined', 'certain' and
the phrase 'could not have done otherwise', and partly
from the 'ghost in the machine' myth, the idea of an 'I',
separate and static, instead of an evolving and changing
personality.

I suggest that the clearest way of thinking about it is
something like this:

All-that-I-am-now is deciding freely (that is without external compulsion) what I am going to do.

This all-that-I-am might have been different if events had happened differently in the past, but it is what it is and, in a sense, it includes the decision that is now being made.

The choices that all-that-I-will-be will make in the future are undecided though they may be correctly predicted. They will depend on what all-that-I-will-be turns out to be like and this will depend on the nature of all-that-I-am-now and on external events.

Smith, being what he was at that moment, could not have behaved other than he did at that moment. What he was at that moment was therefore *responsible* for what he did.

If you approve of what he did, it will be sensible for you to praise him, perhaps to reward him: this will make it more likely that Smith and others will behave in similar ways in the future.

Similarly, if you disapprove of what he did, blame and, if it is within your power, punishment may make similar behaviour in the future less likely.

The increased success with which it is claimed that the causes of behaviour are being discovered, that behaviour is being explained, should not make the notion of responsibility less important. But it should perhaps lead to a greater emphasis on the obvious fact that it is more sensible and useful to think of praise and blame as directed towards modifying future behaviour rather than as a rejoicing in or crying over the accurately poured or carelessly spilt milk of the past.

Exercises

1. 'A man can do what he will, but not will as he will.'

SCHOPENHAUER

Discuss.

2. 'We needs must love the highest when we see it.'

How does this fit into the Determinism–Free Will controversy?

3. BOSWELL: It [a book they were discussing] puzzled me so much as to the freedom of the human will, by stating, with wonderful acute ingenuity, our being actuated by a series of motives which we cannot resist, that the only relief I had was to forget it. . . .

DR JOHNSON: . . . It is certain I am either to go home tonight or not; that does not prevent my freedom.

BOSWELL: That it is certain you are *either* to go home or not, does not prevent your freedom: because the liberty of choice between the two is compatible with that certainty. But if *one* of these events be certain *now*, you have no *future* power of volition. If it be certain you are to go home tonight, you *must* go home. JAMES BOSWELL, *The Life of Dr Johnson*, Vol. II, p. 209.

Do you think Boswell has stated the case correctly or that he is in a bit of a muddle? If so, sort it out.

4. In the following passage from his *The Case for Modern Man* C. Frankel is considering the views of Dr Reinhold Niebuhr. He describes Dr Niebuhr's concept of 'the paradox of human freedom'.

Man is limited, subject to causal necessity, bound to finite conditions. And yet he is also free, able to introduce novelty into the universe, to choose his own path for himself, and to be held responsible for his actions. On one side, man is a mortal creature, put into a world he has not made, and which limits and determines what he does at every turn. On the other side, man is able to transcend the bounds of his creaturely existence. By some strange illogic in the universe he is free and able to overstep his limits. . . . He (Dr Niebuhr) believes that there is a logical paradox in believing that men can be free, and at the same time subject to external causal conditions. . . . What are the logical credentials of this conception of freedom . . . ? (op. cit., p. 84).

What would be your answer to this question?

5. Discuss the argument of the following passage in which H. W. B. Joseph claims to show that Determinism cannot be true:

For the scientific account, though not claiming to be good or right, claims to be true; and it cannot reasonably do this, and abolish the possibility of knowledge.

Yet surely it does abolish this possibility. In the extreme instance of a Behaviouristic account of the mind, that seems obvious; for if thought *is* laryngeal motion, how should anyone think more truly than the wind blows? All movements of bodies are equally necessary, but they cannot be discriminated as true and false. It seems as nonsensical to call a movement true as a flavour purple or a sound avaricious. But what is obvious when thought is said to *be* a certain movement seems equally to follow from its being the effect of one. Thought called knowledge and thought called error are both necessary results of states of brain. These states are necessary results of other bodily states. All the bodily states are equally real, and so are the different thoughts; but by what right can I hold that my thought is knowledge of what is real in bodies? For to hold so is but another thought, an effect of real bodily movements like the rest. An intelligence not determined by what falls within this bodily system to which belong the conditions producing our thoughts might, if it were capable of knowing both the events in that system and the thoughts of it which these determine, discover under what conditions bodily events within the system produce thoughts of it agreeing with what this extraneous intelligence knows it to be, and under what conditions not. But the thought determined by these conditions could not know what the extraneous intelligence knew without being itself also extraneous to the system within which, nevertheless, the conditions determining it are supposed to lie. These arguments, however, of mine, if the principles of scientific theory are to stand unchallenged, are themselves no more than happenings in a mind, results of bodily movements; that you or I think them sound, or think them unsound, is but another such happening; that we think them no more than another such happening is itself but yet another such. And it may be said of any ground on which we may attempt to stand as true, *Labitur et labetur in omne volubilis aevum.*

That the principles, then, on which rests the scientific theory of the world are absolutely true is not only inconsistent with ethical theory: it is inconsistent with there being knowledge, or even true opinion. And therefore with themselves; for they claim to be matter of knowledge, or at least of true opinion. H. W. B. JOSEPH, *Some Problems in Ethics,* pp. 14-15.

Supplementary passages
(1) The following passage makes, perhaps over-emphatically, but picturesquely, the point about the distinction between what is *necessary* and what is *contingent*:

There are certain sequences or developments (cases of one thing following another), which are, in the true sense of the word, reasonable. They are, in the true sense of the word, necessary. Such are mathematical and merely logical sequences. . . . For instance if the Ugly Sisters are older then Cinderella it is (in an iron and awful sense) *necessary* that Cinderella is younger than the Ugly Sisters. . . . But as I . . . began to take notice of the natural world, I observed an extraordinary thing. I observed that learned men in spectacles were talking of the actual things that happened – dawn and death and so on – as if *they* were rational and inevitable. They talked as if the fact that trees bear fruit were just as *necessary* as the fact that two and one trees make three. But it is not. There is an enormous difference by the test ... of imagination. You cannot *imagine* two and one not making three. But you can easily imagine trees not growing fruit; you can imagine them growing golden candlesticks or tigers hanging by the tail. These men in spectacles spoke much of a man named Newton, who was hit by an apple, and who discovered a law. But they could not be got to see the distinction between a true law, a law of reason, and the mere fact of apples falling. If the apple hit Newton's nose, Newton's nose hit the apple. That is a true necessity: because we cannot conceive the one occurring without the other. But we can quite well conceive the apple not falling on his nose. ... G. K. CHESTERTON, *Orthodoxy*, pp. 49, 50.

(2) The following passage from Bergson's *Creative Evolution* expresses the point about the changing 'I'.

What are we, in fact, what is our *character*, if not the condensation of the history that we have lived from our birth – nay, even before our birth, since we bring with us prenatal dispositions? Doubtless we think with only a small part of our past, but it is with our entire past, including the original bent of our soul, that we desire, will and act.

From this survival of the past it follows that consciousness cannot go through the same state twice. The circumstances may still be the same, but they will act no longer on the same person, since they find him at a new moment of his history. Our personality, which is being built up each instant with its accumulated experience changes without ceasing. Op. cit., trans. by A. Mitchell, pp. 5, 6.

1. 'An irrational situation cannot be analysed rationally.'
Discuss.

2. But this priviledge [man's ability to *Reason*], is allayed by
another; and that is by the priviledge of Absurdity; to which
no living creature is subject, but man onely. And of men, those
are of all most subject to it, that professe Philosophy. For it is
most true that *Cicero* sayeth of them somewhere; that there can
be nothing so absurd, but may be found in the books of Philosophers. And the reason is manifest. For there is not one of them
that begins his ratiocination from the Definitions, or Explica-
tions of the names they are to use; which is a method that hath
been used onely in Geometry; whose conclusions have thereby
been made indisputable. THOMAS HOBBES (1588–1679),
Leviathan, Ch. 5.

Discuss this criticism of Philosophers. To what extent do
you think you could defend them against it?

3. Mr Macleod [who had just been appointed Editor of the
Spectator] dismissed the criticism that his own political allegiance would affect the paper's independence as a 'very
strange doctrine'. He added 'If you carry that to its logical
conclusion, the only people fit to be editors would be those who
have no strong views about anything. I cannot regard that as a
good qualification'. *The Times*, 8 November 1963.

(The following is an extract from a statement by the
board of the paper which was printed earlier in the same
column:

'Independence does not mean that the paper should not
have strong political views. True independence means that

the paper's views are not dictated from outside its office.')

Discuss the way in which the word 'independence' is used.

What unstated premisses does the 'logical conclusion' require?

4. 'Wisdom brings happiness; no wise man therefore can be unhappy.'

Discuss.

5. Since he was a philosopher by profession I asked him to explain something that I had never been able to understand. I asked him whether the statement that two and two make four means anything. I couldn't see that four was anything but a convenient synonym for two and two. If you look out *violent* in Roget you will see that there are something like fifty synonyms for it; they have different associations and some by the number of their syllables, the collocation of their letters or the difference of their sound may be more suitable for use in a particular sentence than others, but they all *mean* the same thing. Roughly, of course, for no synonym is quite precise; and four may be a synonym not only for two and two, but for three and one and for one and one and one and one. My philosopher said he thought the statement that two and two make four had a definite meaning, but he didn't seem able to tell me exactly what it was; and when I asked him whether mathematics was ultimately anything more than an immensely elaborate Roget's *Thesaurus* he changed the conversation. W. SOMERSET MAUGHAM, *A Writer's Notebook*, p. 253.

What answer would you make to Somerset Maugham's inquiry?

6. Johnson was present when a tragedy was read, in which there occurred this line:

'Who rules o'er freemen should himself be free.'

The company having admired it much, 'I cannot agree with you (said Johnson). It might as well be said, 'Who drives fat oxen should himself be fat.' BOSWELL, *The Life of Dr Johnson*, Vol. II, p. 535.

Do you agree with Johnson that 'it might as well be said'? Explain why, or why not.

7. Has a single individual the right to possess and keep for his own enjoyment works of art which are part of the cultural heritage of mankind? The fact that I cannot phrase this question without employing clichés, suggests that it has about it an element of humbug. SIR KENNETH CLARK, article about Great Private Collections, *Sunday Times*, 22 September 1963.

Analyse the way in which the words 'clichés' and 'humbug' are being used here. Do you think his suggested conclusion is reasonable?

8. Strange it is, that men should admit the validity of the arguments for free discussion, but object to their being 'pushed to an extreme'; not seeing that unless the reasons are good for an extreme case, they are not good for any case. J. S. MILL, *On Liberty*, p. 83.

Do you agree that, as far as free discussion is concerned, 'unless the reasons are good for an extreme case, they are not good for any case'?

Discuss the general application of this same principle, for example, with regard to Generosity, Tolerance, Nationalization, Temperance.

9. Consider to what extent the following statements are capable of verification or falsification.

i. Always by the event, and most often, when history does not fail us, by their lives, we know that the greatest artists were the sanest men of their generation. E. F. CARRITT, *The Theory of Beauty*, p. 8.

ii. No word is more frequently or loosely used than the word 'freedom'.

iii. All the ideals of human behaviour formulated by those who have been most successful in freeing themselves from the prejudices of their time and place are singularly alike. ALDOUS HUXLEY, *Ends and Means*, p. 2.

10. For the effect must correspond to its cause, and is even best known by knowledge of its cause, and it is unreasonable to introduce a sovereign intelligence ordering all things and then, instead of using his wisdom, only to use the properties of matter to explain phenomena. As if, to account for the victory of a great Prince in taking some important stronghold, an historian were to say that it was because the corpuscles of gunpowder, being released at the touch of a spark, escaped with a speed capable of throwing a hard heavy body against the walls of the stronghold, while the branches of the corpuscles which make up the copper of the cannon were so well interlaced as not to tear asunder by this speed; instead of showing how the foresight of the victor made him choose the suitable time and means, and how his power surmounted all obstacles. G. W. LEIBNIZ, *Discourse on Metaphysics*, trans. by P. G. Lucas and L. Grint, p. 34.

Elucidate the two methods of 'explaining phenomena' referred to here.

11. The hand, to be sure, does not seem to be such a very external thing for fate; it seems rather to stand to it as something inner. For fate again is also merely the phenomenal manifestation of what the specifically determinate individuality inherently is as having an inner determinate constitution originally and

from the start. Now to find out what this individuality is in itself, the palmist, as well as the physiognomist, takes a shorter cut than, e.g. Solon, who thought he could only know this from and after the course of the whole life: the latter looked at the phenomenal explicit reality, while the former considers the implicit nature (*das Ansich*). That the hand, however, must exhibit and reveal the inherent nature of individuality as regards its fate, is easily seen from the fact that after the organ of speech it is the hand most of all by which a man actualizes and manifests himself. It is the lively artificer of his fortune: we may say of the hand it *is* what a man does, for in it as the effective organ of his self-fulfilment he is there present as the animating soul; and since he is ultimately and originally his own fate, the hand will thus express this innate inherent nature. G. W. F. HEGEL, *The Phenomenology of Mind*, trans. by J. B. Baillie, p. 303.

What, very briefly, is being said here? Do you think that the 'must' which occurs about half way through the passage is a logical must? If so, do the premisses justify the conclusion?

12. Consider the following:

i. What can be a more extreme absurdity than that of proposing to improve social life by breaking the fundamental law of social life. H. SPENCER, *Principles of Ethics*, Vol. II, p. 260.
ii. The principles of an organized society cannot be interpreted in practice in such a way as to make organized society impossible. J. BURNHAM, *The Struggle for the World*, p. 211.

The 'fundamental law' referred to in (i) is that of the survival of the fittest. The main principle referred to in (ii) is free speech. Develop each argument and consider to what extent they are in conflict with each other.

13. But it is liberty to know oneself; and by transcendence of knowledge to be oneself; and by penetration of being to lose oneself; and in losing, find. C. MORGAN, *Liberties of the Mind*, p. 65.

Discuss.

14. Consider the argument of the following passage:

There are, as you probably know, some philosophers who insist strongly on a doctrine which they express by saying that no relations are purely external. And so far as I can make out one thing which they mean by this is just that whenever x has any relation whatever which y has not got, x and y *cannot* be exactly alike; that any difference in relation necessarily entails a difference in intrinsic nature. There is, I think, no doubt that when these philosophers say this, they mean by their 'cannot' and 'necessarily' an unconditional 'cannot' and 'must'. And hence it follows they are holding that, if, for instance, a thing A pleases me now, then any other thing, B, precisely similar to A, must under any circumstances, and in any Universe, please me also: since, if B did not please me, it would *not* possess a relation which A does possess, and therefore, by their principle, *could* not be precisely similar to A – *must* differ from it in intrinsic nature. But it seems to me to be obvious that this principle is false. If it were true, it would follow that I can know *a priori* such things as that no patch of colour which is seen by you and is not seen by me is ever exactly like any patch which is seen by me and is not seen by you: or that no patch of colour which is surrounded by a red ring is ever exactly like one which is not so surrounded. But it is surely obvious that, whether these things are true or not they are things which I cannot know *a priori*. It is simply *not* evident *a priori* that no patch of colour which is seen by A and not by B is ever exactly like one which is seen by B and not by A, and that no patch of colour which is surrounded by a red ring is ever exactly like one which is not. And this illustration serves to bring out very well both what is meant by saying of such a predicate as 'beautiful' that it is 'intrinsic' and why, if it is, it cannot be subjective. What is meant is just that if A is beautiful and B is not, you could know *a priori* that A and B are *not* exactly alike; whereas, with any such subjective predicate, as that of exciting a particular feeling in me, or that of being a thing which would excite such a feeling in any spectator, you cannot tell *a priori* that a thing A which did possess such a predicate and a thing B which did not, could not be exactly alike.

It seems to me, therefore, quite certain, in spite of the dogma that no relations are purely external, that there are many predicates, such for instance as most (if not all) subjective predicates or the objective one of being surrounded by a red ring, which do *not* depend solely on the intrinsic nature of what possesses them: or, in other words, of which it is *not* true that if *x* possesses them and *y* does not, *x* and *y* *must* differ in intrinsic nature. But what precisely is meant by this unconditional 'must', I must confess I don't know. The obvious thing to suggest is that it is the logical 'must', which certainly is unconditional in just this sense: the kind of necessity, which we assert to hold, for instance, when we say that whatever is a right-angled triangle *must* be a triangle, or that whatever is yellow *must* be either yellow or blue. But I must say I cannot see that all unconditional necessity is of this nature. I do not see how it can be deduced from any logical law that, if a given patch of colour be yellow, then any patch which were exactly like the first would be yellow too. And similarly in our case of 'intrinsic' value, though I think it is true that beauty, for instance, is 'intrinsic' I, do not see how it can be deduced from any logical law, that if A is beautiful anything that were exactly like A would be beautiful too, in exactly the same degree. G. E. MOORE, *Philosophical Studies*, Routledge, pp. 270–72, (from an essay on 'The Conception of Intrinsic Value').

'Intrinsic' Value has been defined earlier in the essay as follows:

To say that a kind of value is 'intrinsic' means merely that the question whether a thing possesses it, and in what degree it possesses it, depends solely on the intrinsic nature of the thing in question. Ibid. p. 260.

15. Descartes (1596–1650) was a famous mathematician as well as a philosopher. His philosophical method was one of systematically refusing to accept any proposition of which he could not be certain. He came to the conclusion, however, that there was one basic truth which he could not doubt.

'... I observed that, whilst I thus wished to think that all was false, it was absolutely necessary that I, who thus thought, should be somewhat; and as I observed that this truth, *I think hence I am*, was so certain and of such evidence, that no ground of doubt however extravagant, could be alleged by the sceptics capable of shaking it, I concluded that I might, without scruple, accept it as the first principle of the philosophy of which I was in search. *A Discourse on Method*, Part IV, pp. 26, 27.

A few paragraphs later he goes on to say:

In the next place, from reflecting on the circumstance that I doubted, and that consequently my being was not wholly perfect (for I clearly saw that it was a greater perfection to know than to doubt), I was led to inquire whence I had learned to think of something more perfect than myself; and I clearly recognized that I must hold this notion from some nature which in reality was more perfect. As for the thoughts of many other objects external to me, as of the sky, the earth, light, heat and a thousand more, I was less at a loss to know whence these came; for since I remarked in them nothing which seemed to render them superior to myself, I could believe that, if these were true, they were dependencies on my own nature, insofar as it possessed a certain perfection, and, if they were false, that I held them from nothing, that is to say, that they were in me because of a certain imperfection of my nature. But this could not be the case with the idea of a nature more perfect than myself; for to receive it from nothing was a thing manifestly impossible; and, because it is not less repugnant that the more perfect should be an effect of, and dependence on the less perfect, than that something should proceed from nothing, it was equally impossible that I could hold it from myself: accordingly, it but remained that it had been placed in me by a nature which was in reality more perfect than mine, and which even possessed within itself all the perfections of which I could form any idea; that is to say, in a single word, which was God.

Discuss and analyse the idea of 'perfection' which seems to be implicit in this passage. Do you think the argument is a valid demonstration of the existence of God?

16. If thou shouldst say, 'It is enough, I have reached perfection', all is lost. For it is the function of perfection to make one know one's imperfection. ST AUGUSTINE, quoted by Aldous Huxley, *The Perennial Philosophy*, p. 334.

Do you think Descartes would have accepted this (see Exercise 15)? And if so, would he have had to say that God knew he was imperfect?

17. In his essay *On Liberty* J. S. Mill (1806–73) is arguing that one reason why there should be liberty of thought and discussion is that to suppress opinions which are thought to be erroneous assumes that the individual or the age is infallible, an assumption which is contrary to historical experience. ('every age having held many opinions which subsequent ages have deemed not only false but absurd.')

He goes on:

The objection likely to be made to this argument would probably take some such form as the following. There is no greater assumption of infallibility in forbidding the propagation of error, than in any other thing which is done by public authority on its own judgement and responsibility. Judgement is given to men that they may use it. Because it may be used erroneously, are men to be told that they ought not to use it at all? To prohibit what they think pernicious, is not claiming exemption from error, but fulfilling the duty incumbent on them, although fallible, of acting on their conscientious conviction. If we were never to act on our opinions, because those opinions may be wrong, we should leave all our interests uncared for, and all our duties unperformed. An objection which applies to all conduct can be no valid objection to any conduct in particular. It is the duty of governments, and of individuals, to form the truest opinions they can; to form them carefully, and never impose them upon others unless they are quite sure of being right. But when they are sure (such reasoners may say), it is not conscientiousness but cowardice to shrink from acting on their opinions, and allow doctrines which they honestly think dangerous to the welfare of mankind, either in this life or in another, to be scattered abroad without restraint, because other people, in less enlightened times have persecuted opinions now believed to be true. Let us take care, it may be said, not to make the same mistake: but governments and nations have made mistakes in other things, which are not denied to be fit subjects for the exercise of authority: they have laid on bad taxes, made unjust wars. Ought we therefore to lay on no taxes, and, under whatever provocation, make no wars? Men, and governments, must act to the best of their ability. There is no such thing as absolute certainty, but there is assurance sufficient for the purposes of human life. We may, and must, assume our opinion to be true for the guidance of our own conduct: and it is assuming no more when we forbid bad men to pervert society by the propagation of opinions which we regard as false and pernicious. Op. cit., pp. 80–81.

Summarize this argument and discuss its validity. Mill's next paragraph starts 'I answer. . . .' What sort of answer would you expect him to make?

18. In the passage from Bergson's *Creative Evolution* quoted on page 67 there is a reference to the arrow of Zeno. Zeno was a philosopher of the fifth century B.C. who propounded various paradoxes. The one about the arrow is stated by Bergson thus:

Take the flying arrow. At every moment, says Zeno, it is motionless, for it cannot have time to move, that is, to occupy at least two successive positions, unless at least two moments are allowed it. At a given moment, therefore, it is at rest at a given point. Motionless in each point of its course, it is motionless during all the time that it is moving. *Creative Evolution*, p. 325.

Discuss this paradox with particular reference to the passage on page 67.

19. In the following passage from *The Problems of Philosophy* Russell claims to prove that there are such things as Universals. Do you think he succeeds?

As a matter of fact, if anyone were anxious to deny altogether that there are such things as universals, we should find that we cannot strictly prove that there are such entities as *qualities*, i.e. the universals represented by adjectives and substantives, whereas we can prove that there must be *relations*, i.e. the sort of universals generally represented by verbs and prepositions. Let us take in illustration the universal *whiteness*. If we believe that there is such a universal, we shall say that things are white because they have the quality of whiteness. This view, however, was strenuously denied by Berkeley and Hume, who have been followed in this by later empiricists. The form which their denial took was to deny that there are such things as 'abstract ideas'. When we want to think of whiteness, they said, we form an image of some particular white thing, and reason concerning this particular, taking care not to deduce anything concerning it which we cannot see to be equally true of any other white thing. As an account of our actual mental processes, this is no doubt largely true. In geometry, for example, when we wish to prove something about all triangles, we draw a particular triangle and reason about it, taking care not to use any characteristic which it does not share with other triangles. The beginner, in order to avoid error, often finds it useful to draw several triangles, as unlike each other as possible, in order to make sure that his reasoning is equally applicable to all of them. But a difficulty emerges as soon as we ask ourselves how we know that a thing is white or a triangle. If we wish to avoid the universals *whiteness* and *triangularity*, we shall choose some particular patch of white or some particular triangle, and say that anything is white or a triangle if it has the right sort of resemblance to our chosen particular. But then the resemblance required will have to be a universal. Since there are many white things, the resemblance must hold between many pairs of particular white things; and this is the characteristic of a universal. It will be useless to say that there is a different resemblance for each pair, for then we shall have to say that these resemblances resemble each other, and thus at last we shall be forced to admit resemblance as a universal. The relation of resemblance, therefore, must be a true universal. And having been forced to admit this universal, we find that it is no longer worth while to invent difficult and unplausible theories to avoid the admission of such universals as whiteness and triangularity. BERTRAND RUSSELL, *The Problems of Philosophy*, pp. 95-7.

COMMENTS ON EXERCISES

CHAPTER 2

2. (*a*) i. Identically the same.

ii. Different but exactly alike. (It is possible but improbable that the ladies took it in turns to wear identically the same hat.)

(The sameness of (i) is sometimes called 'quantitative' and of (ii) 'qualitative'.)

iii. Rather loosely similar; general principles having important points of resemblance.

iv. The system of rules and regulations which is in print has not been changed since last year.

(*b*) i. 'has the property of being'

ii. 'is equal to'

(Notice that these two phrases are not in general interchangeable.)

(*c*) i. good faith = honesty, integrity

ii. beliefs, probably religious

iii. confidence

(*d*) i. To call X a 'real cricketer' would probably be to commend him as a cricketer, to say that he was good at cricket. But how can one be good at smoking? 'real' here seems to be intended just to imply status or prestige; not to be a real smoker would somehow be debased, unworthy.

ii. as opposed to imaginary; its existence would be verified by the other senses.

iii. the *important* or *difficult* problem

(*e*) i. A slightly odd use. Possibly something rather more than 'purpose' intended; if so perhaps a rather mystical something.

ii. A look that was intended to convey information, or do some of the other things that language does.

iii. Purpose, significance

iv. Importance, significance, how it is related to other things, possible causes and effects etc.

v. The English equivalents

3. 'The perfect use of language' referred to in the first sentence implies and necessitates agreement between those who use the words and those to whom the meaning is carried. It is clearly absurd to claim (and impossible to prove) that there can ever have been a time when this agreement was complete. But there may well have been a period when usages were unusually simple (a reaction from 'metaphysical conceits') and generally agreed.

'Impossible to write badly': the most that one could claim would be that because of the simple and generally agreed usages it was exceptionally easy to convey one's meaning accurately. It might be said that 'impossible' was being used here in such a way as to depreciate the currency.

4. Analogies may be useful and illuminating up to a point, but they should be used no further than 'suits purposes' and they do not have logical conclusions. Words bear a resemblance to chisels in that they are both, in a sense, tools. But they are basically dissimilar. The chisel has a physical existence apart from its use and its name; this remains approximately unchanged. A word has no physical existence and, as has been pointed out in this chapter, it means what it is used to mean.

5. Task of philosopher to examine and analyse concepts being used by scientists and others. Important for him to point out that entities are invented by man and should be used,

in this awareness, only in so far as they are useful. As with all analogies it is dangerous to take them too far. Much philosophizing in the past has been undertaken with concepts – e.g. of 'mind' – whose use is now thought by some not to be helpful. Helpful for what? In the long run for clearer thinking and better, fuller living. Which is what all philosophizing must eventually be for. The trouble is that the length of the run may make the test of usefulness very difficult to apply in practice.

10. i. No doubt about (b). The answer is: 'This set of words is a sentence.' (a) looks a bit trickier. If it was said about another sentence there would be no doubt what was meant: that it was a proper sentence (with subject, verb, predicate), and was intelligible. The claim here is the same, but it really hardly says anything. 'What sense?' can only be answered by repeating the sentence and adding some such comment as the above.

ii. Definition of 'pain' blurred. Suppose someone takes my hand and squeezes it with a gradually increasing pressure. When do I say it becomes painful? When I start not to like it? Do we mean by someone who has never felt pain a person who has never felt pressures etc. or one who has never disliked them? If the latter we might feel that we could explain 'pain' to him if he has ever disliked anything. But if we had someone who had never felt anything or never disliked anything or both, our task would be hopeless. Would this be a man?

'A man could not imagine . . . etc.' How do we know? We could only *know* that it is always true if it is true of necessity, by definition. Otherwise there might always be an exception we haven't met (a man who *could* imagine etc.) Evidence in any case unreliable, we could only have the man's word for it.

iii. Obviously merely verbal. Whether the picture is right or wrong depends on what it's supposed to be, what someone actually sees or what someone might see in different circumstances. In talking of a white rose in the dark we mean a rose that would look white if it wasn't dark.

iv. I think I can do it: certainly with a bit of practice. 'mean' here must refer to what, non-verbally, one has in mind; what one is trying to communicate. Perhaps one could do it either by removing one's attention from the words one is saying, or by keeping the words in mind but investing the word 'cold' with the different meaning.

11. (a) Whitehead's point is that even though Mr Johnson may not have intended to use the term Proposition in twenty different ways (and might indeed deny that he had done so) the fact that another logician can understand twenty different meanings shows that the word could be used in logical contexts in twenty different ways. Twenty new terms (or just *nineteen*?) might therefore be required. But one would rather like to know what Mr Johnson would have said; after all it is not the words that mean, but the person who uses them.

There is the implication that Mr Johnson's argument may have been adversely affected. Whether it was or not, *unnoted* distinctions of this kind clearly could be exceedingly misleading and might therefore matter very much.

11. (b) Mill goes on:

All the inquiries into the *summum bonum* in the philosophical schools were infected with the same fallacy; the ambiguous word being, as before, Evil, or its contrary correlative, Good, which sometimes meant what is good for one's self, at other times what is good for other people. That nothing which is a cause of evil on the whole to other people, can be really good for the agent himself, is indeed a possible tenet, and always a favourite one with moralists, although in the present age the question has rather been, not whether the proposition is true, but how society and education can be so ordered as to make it true. At all events, it is not proved merely by the fact that a thing beneficial to the world, and a thing beneficial to a person himself, are both in common parlance called *good*. That is no valid argument, but a fallacy of ambiguity.

13. Austin goes on to consider the three sentences as follows:

We would say the first of these things simply by way of commenting on his *looks* – he has the look of a guilty man. The second, I suggest, would typically be used with reference to certain *special circumstances* – 'I quite agree that, when he's prevaricating over all those searching questions about what he did with the money, he appears guilty, but most of the time his demeanour [not just "his looks"] is innocence itself'. And the third, fairly clearly, makes an implicit reference to certain *evidence* – evidence bearing, of course, on the question whether he *is* guilty, though not such as to settle that question conclusively – 'On the evidence we've heard so far, he certainly seems guilty.' J. L. AUSTIN, *Sense and Sensibilia*, pp. 36, 37.

CHAPTER 3

5. 'Utilitarian' is sometimes used in a narrow, disapproving sense when applied to education, meaning useful for making a living, often in a humdrum unacademic way. But of course all education should have as its objective the

making of better citizens in the widest sense of 'better', and what is this if not utilitarian?

6. The *Shorter O.E.D.* gives 'improvement or refinement by education and training'. Sir Charles Snow, who wrote about the concept of two cultures, said that in his title the word had two meanings. For the first he gives the dictionary definition and also Coleridge's 'the harmonious development of those qualities and faculties which characterize our humanity'. For the second he says 'It [the word 'culture'] is used by anthropologists to denote a group of persons living in the same environment, linked by common habits, common assumptions, a common way of life.' (*The Times Literary Supplement*, 25 October 1963.)

The writer of the article seems to be using the word sometimes in one sense, sometimes in the other. Some confusion seems to result from this.

8. Perfect for what? One can of course *define* 'perfect' as applied to plane figures so that the circle is necessarily the most perfect, and one can make 'the most perfect' mean something for some other purposes. But on the whole the idea of abstract, absolute perfection does not seem to be a useful concept; we generally want to use the word in a relative, limited way. (See also pages 235, 236.)

9. Hayek goes on:

To the great apostles of political freedom the word had meant freedom from coercion, freedom from the arbitrary power of other men, release from the ties which left the individual no choice but obedience to the orders of a superior to whom he was attached. The new freedom promised, however, was to be freedom from necessity, release from the compulsion of the circumstances which inevitably limit the range of choice. . . .

Before man could be truly free, the 'despotism of physical want' had to be broken, the 'restraints of the economic system' relaxed.

Freedom in this sense is, of course, merely another name for power or wealth. . . . The demand for the new freedom was thus only another name for the old demand for an equal distribution of wealth. *The Road to Serfdom*, p. 19.

10. The following points might be made:

i. 'Progress' today is used on the whole to refer to changes that are considered improvements. Opinions may therefore differ as to whether an actual or proposed change constitutes progress. The adjective or noun 'progressive' however is sometimes used in a pejorative sense about those who want change of a certain kind.

ii. Spencer seems to take the view that there is a true essential meaning, what Progress is 'in itself'. It is his aim to find this. He finds it in the evolution of the homogeneous (of one kind) into the heterogeneous (of many kinds).

iii. There are here two separate questions. The first is whether we in fact find a tendency for Society, Government etc. to evolve from the simple into the complex, from the less varied into the more varied. The answer must be that we do. Look around and see. The second question should surely be whether on the whole we use the word 'Progress' to apply to this process or whether we shall agree to do so. Spencer might be criticized for asking the wrong question here, for taking too rigid a view of the meaning of a word.

CHAPTER 4

1. i. Answerable in principle and practice to any degree of accuracy that is likely to be required.

ii. Answerable in principle – there must be an answer. Unlikely to be answerable in practice at all accurately; not many people would know with precision how heavy they were two years ago.

iii. Certainly not answerable, except very vaguely, in practice. And it is not really answerable even in principle; there *is* no answer that is anything like precise. One can make some interesting comparisons of the sorts of things one could buy with a pound 300 years ago and what one can buy now, but most of these things will be very different and a comparison of values for periods so far apart does not mean much.

iv. Even without taking 'whole truth' very literally it could hardly be claimed that this is answerable in practice. The 'whole truth' would presumably include everything he has ever done, every thought he has ever had, every influence to which he has been subjected, all about these influences and so on. It might be argued that the whole truth in this sense is unlimited and cannot therefore be known even in principle, but this is a partly verbal question.

v. More limited than (iv). For any purposes for which the question is likely to be asked probably answerable in principle, though quite likely not in practice.

vi. In a sense unanswerable both in principle and practice because there can be no precise answer. It occurs an indefinitely, or infinitely, large number of times.

2. i. Probably entirely verbal. It looks as though the questioner did not know until this moment what aquamarine looked like.

ii. Could be the same as (i) but unlikely. It looks more like a rebuke, with a sarcastic inflexion.

iii. Question might be: 'How do we use the word science?', or 'Are the methods of Economics sufficiently systematic, and the conclusions sufficiently definite?', or a mixture of both.

iv. Almost bound to be a question of just how the words 'unreasonable' and 'irrational' are used.

v. Most people would probably have a sufficiently clear idea how they use the words to answer 'Yes' without hesitation. Any doubt there was would be likely to revolve around the use of 'wise'.

vi. Almost certainly verbal.

vii. Probably hardly at all verbal. We know well enough what it is to be conceited and happy.

viii. Verbal.

ix. Very unlikely to be verbal. The questioner probably wants to know about their specifications, mechanical details, etc.

x. Almost certainly verbal. How are the words 'banter' and 'badinage' used?

xi. Probably partly verbal. Just where shall we draw the line between them? What about the psalms, etc? Also what are their characteristics?

xii. Unlikely to be verbal. 'Meaning' in the sense of 'purpose'.

3. i. An answer might be given in terms of a creator's plan or purpose, but this would be unlikely to satisfy. A biologist might be able to give reasons why an animal with three legs would not survive, and such an answer would probably be acceptable. The answer might be that they just haven't.

ii. Questioner probably just wondering. *Is* it only

convention? What *caused* the convention? Has it a *purpose*? To start the week well by getting clean?

iii. Possible answers expected: an explanation of what he has done; an explanation of the purpose – to stop him and others from doing it again; pointing out that it is our custom to punish people who do that. The question might imply 'was it really necessary . . . ?'

iv. This looks like a *basic* moral question. The answer might be: we just *should*, because it's *right*. Or it might be an explanation that society can't function properly unless we agree to keep our promises.

v. This looks like a complaint and a reprimand. There may well not be much opportunity for answering.

vi. He sounds tired. The acceptable answer would no doubt be the last line of the poem:

'O, rest ye, brother mariners, we will not wander more'.

vii. This might be a complaint. An answer might be (*a*) because the chauffeur's ill (antecedent cause); or (*b*) so that we can go out in it this evening (purpose).

viii. A complaint.

4. Comments on these questions can be made more briefly by using 'boo-word' and 'hurrah-word' to indicate words which are generally used to indicate disapproval and approval respectively. For example 'liberty' might be used as a hurrah-word and 'licence' as a boo-word for an absence of constraint.

i. It's unlikely that the questioner is. 'Doctrinaire' almost always a boo-word. 'Egalitarianism' usually is: corresponding hurrah-word, 'equality'.

ii. and iii. Stuart Chase (*The Proper Study of Mankind*, pp. 162–3) describes a test where these two questions were put to similar groups of people and received

significantly different answers. The implication being
that 'propaganda' is a boo-word for 'our point of view'.
It might be argued, however, that people understand by
'propaganda' an inaccurate or misleading statement of
a point of view.

iv. 'Sweat' and 'fritter' very much boo-words. The main
point of our exports is to enable us to pay for our imports,
especially food.

v. 'Materialistic' a boo-word to describe a high standard
of living. 'Leisured age' often a euphemism for a time
when a minority had more leisure, but the majority
worked much harder.

5. i. That *we* form a superior élite, probably social.

ii. That the mind can sensibly be thought of as a separate
entity to which spatial metaphors are applicable. (It may
well be the case that if 'brain' were substituted for
'mind' this would be a perfectly proper question, to
which the answer is being found.)

iii. That envy, hatred, malice can be regarded as separate
sins to which degrees of wickedness can be attached, as
though one were considering which was the heaviest of
three stones.

6. They are all so hopelessly vague that one hardly knows
where to start. Ideally one would want to be able to ask the
questioner just what it is that he wants to know and for
what purpose.

i. Which women? Where? When? Better in what way?

ii. Criteria wanted for being 'truly educated'. But one
might describe the distinctive features of the educated
classic and scientist and leave it to the questioner to
decide which he calls more truly educated.

iii. 'Significant' in a vacuum almost meaningless. For

what ? For the progress or happiness of mankind ? What counts as a cultural activity ? Anything that's encouraged by education ?

iv. Presumably a religious or moral question. *Ought* all men to treat each other like brothers ?

v. Presumably more important for the benefit of the community. Would we prefer a society in which more emphasis is placed on J. or on F. ? Is it implied that they are in any sense alternatives ? Are they ? Think of *people* being treated justly, and of *people* being free from restraint.

7. i. The built-in answer is that it is impossible. We can never be 'in' any moment except the present.

ii. An entirely verbal question. It depends what one means by 'think'.

iii. This question needs some sorting out. Mostly dependent on whether we think that stupidity is avoidable. Arguable that almost anybody can to some extent behave less stupidly, do fewer silly things, get more sums right, etc. by taking care, by trying. View might be taken that everyone has a certain unalterable 'amount' of intelligence and therefore of stupidity. Difficult to uphold this view.

iv. Entirely verbal. What are we going to mean by 'upstairs' and 'downstairs'.

v. In a sense, nowhere. If anyone is genuinely puzzled about this the most satisfactory answer would probably be the scientific one: ' It looks as though it's there because . . . rays of light . . . etc.'

vi. This depends very much on who is asking it, at what level and for what purpose. In the beginnings of Arithmetic the answer would be short with a practical demonstration, perhaps using fingers. At a deeper or a higher level many volumes have been written about the concept of number.

vii. Entirely verbal. How are we using 'same' and 'different'?

CHAPTER 5

1. It all depends: 'Better than' is used to mean different things in different contexts. The fact (or opinion) that A is better than B in one respect and B better than C in another would tell us nothing at all about the comparative merits of A and C in any respect.

3. What is meant seems to be something like this: 'For the decision to be determined, or even influenced, by financial considerations (money values) means really that it will be determined . . . etc. by something that is not important (is of no value, or is not a *real* value).' 'Value' is being used in rather different senses to achieve an epigrammatic effect.

How important financial considerations should be is obviously a matter of opinion. Probably not many people would think that they should carry no weight, but it seems perfectly reasonable to hope that the decision 'will not be determined by finance alone'.

5. Can one have a preference or desire of which one is ignorant? And if so, is it likely to lead to action? Surely the consumer will buy those things which he is conscious of desiring. But perhaps the consumer does not predict accurately what he *will* desire, what his acts of choice will be. The advertising agency may claim to discover by investigation whether this is true, but if the consumer is going to be informed by advertisement about all the wants he didn't know he had, the conclusions will not be very convincing.

7. (*a*) This merely says that what we *find* comfortable *is* comfortable for us; that comfort is relative, subjective.

(*b*) What about the subjectivity of sublimity? 'Sublime' is a word of wide meanings, but in one sense at least, that of inspiring awe, reverence, it would certainly seem reasonable to say that what we find sublime is sublime for us.

8. The 'hazel-switch' assumes that there are gems of artistic merit *there* – clearly an objective view. The 'birch twig' assumes that there are certain principles which artists ought to follow: the objectivist and subjectivist could both agree with this – the former would say 'in order to achieve works of merit', the latter, 'in order to make it more likely that people will appreciate your work'.

11. If the marks for the different subjects are added up, perhaps after being scaled to adjust the 'weights' of the subjects, the answer is obviously, Yes. If the final order were produced by adding the places in the different subjects or, what amounts to the same thing, adding the marks after they had been scaled with equal spacing over equal ranges, it might at first appear that no *cardinal* evaluation had taken place. But this procedure makes the assumption that the amount by which A is better than B is equal to the amount by which B is better than C, and so on. In other words it can be argued that a cardinal evaluation of some sort is inevitably implicit in the process.

12. The 'subjectivist' would agree with this fact, but would say that it is not the result of his interpretation but a fact of experience. The very same kind of thing *is* found to be better for certain purposes and in certain circumstances and worse in others, using 'better' very widely and in almost

any sense in which it is likely to be used. It might be objected that some of the judgements about finding it better are just wrong, that its intrinsic value is a matter of fact. This would seem to lead to the conclusion that everything can be arranged on a scale of intrinsic value, with regard, for example, to its beauty; that everything is more or less beautiful than or exactly as beautiful as, every other thing. Many people find this conclusion repugnant to common sense.

13. A difficult question, but interesting to think about. We compare the degrees of our own happiness at different times, but often without much conviction. Scientists might tell us that the state which we call happiness is accompanied by some physical change in the body and that this can be measured and compared for different people. Degrees of happiness might then be quantitatively defined. If Smith and Jones both say that Smith is happier than Jones, if Jones is willing to change places with Smith but not vice versa, then we can agree to describe the situation by saying that Smith is happier than Jones. But if there is no scientific test and if they both say they are very happy, what does it *mean* to say that one is happier? What possible criteria can there be? Is it a question to which there is an answer?

14. The implication is that there is always a clear-cut set of properties defining a concept, and that it is a matter of fact whether a particular example 'fulfils the definition'. This can perhaps be made true for a concept such as 'chair', though even here all sorts of difficulties arise. I call this chair good because I find it comfortable, you call it bad because you don't. It seems that one of us must be wrong and the other right. Does this theory, then, give a satisfactory account of our value judgements?

When one comes to consider the properties that define the concept 'picture' and therefore whether a particular picture 'fulfils its definition' the situation seems even more difficult.

CHAPTER 6

2. Size only frightening by contrast with what is expected or customary. However cows see the external world, including other cows, they presumably always have seen them the same way. Drops in eyes making external world look larger than usual might be an explanation of timorous behaviour, but not a regular 'looking larger than they really are', whatever that may mean.

5. Obviously no answer to this question. Apparent size of objects always relative. Consider how we estimate sizes by comparing proportion of visual field taken up by objects, making allowance for distance away . . . etc.

7. The first sentence seems just to make Berkeley's point: that table exists for me, as I perceive it. The second sentence seems to be about the imagination: however hellish the situation in which one finds oneself the imagination is powerful enough to transform it. These two points seem to be basically different. The first sentence does not seem to suggest that we *create* what we perceive as, in a sense, the imagination does. The third sentence seems to make the same point as the second: the imaginative power of poetry enables us to ignore the external world.

It is interesting to speculate whether Shelley intended in the first sentence to imply that what happens when we perceive things is similar to what happens when the poet uses his imagination.

8. i. To say that a table is related to an experience in precisely the same way as an experience is related to an experience must surely imply that a table and an experience are things of the same kind. But Moore holds the view that a table is a 'material thing in space'.

ii. Perhaps rather misleading to think of an experience as an entity. Does it make sense to say 'my experience can exist, even when I do not happen to be aware of its existence'?

iii. Existence of material objects generally thought to be at best inferred from our sensation.

CHAPTER 7

1. This is rather suggestive of the 'Ghost-in-the-Machine'. A man can do whatever he, his Ghost-in-the-Machine, his Will, decides. But the man-that-wills, the whole of the personality, wills as he does because he is what he is; there is no further ghostly figure inside him. It has been suggested that it is misleading to think of a man-doing as separate from the man-willing inside him.

2. What this seems to say is that our nature is such that when we see, for example, beautiful objects or highly moral conduct we will be strongly attracted. What is 'the highest' is very much a matter of opinion, but as an empirical generalization the statement would probably command fairly general agreement. It is not likely to be used to imply that our actions or emotions are determined and our wills are not free.

3. Dr Johnson goes on to say:

If I am well acquainted with a man, I can judge with great probability how he will act in any case, without his being restrained by my judging. God may have this probability increased to certainty.

'Certainty' is of course the difficulty. The certainty that Dr Johnson is either to go home or not is logical necessity. But *one* of these events cannot in that sense be 'certain' now, though it may well be 'actuated by a series of motives which we cannot resist'. It is a muddle of the kind that confuses *necessary, caused* and *predictable*.

4. Frankel answers the question thus:

It involves a fundamental mistake. For the question of whether an action is determined by external conditions or not has nothing at all to do with whether it is free. The difference between unfree behaviour and free behaviour is not a difference between behaviour that has external causes and behaviour that does not. It is a difference between being coerced and having some choice about the conditions that govern one's behaviour.

He goes on to contrast a totalitarian election and a free election. In the first case the minds of the voters are influenced by such factors as the fear of the police; in the second case they are influenced by considerations such as the existing economic conditions and the policies of the opposing parties. In both cases the mind of the voter is *determined* by certain external conditions.

'Mr Niebuhr's paradox of freedom,' says Frankel, 'confuses freedom with chaos and causation with fate.'

5. Joseph says it is nonsensical to call a movement true, and no doubt he would say that it is not movements that are true but ideas or propositions. But a movement, whether it is mechanically caused or not, can express ideas or propositions and convey information that is true or false. Talking computers can say things to each other that are true or false

and can be made to react appropriately. Notice carefully the use of the word 'determine'; consider where it can be replaced by 'cause' and whether this will make any difference to how convincing the argument is. Is he just saying that a thought that is caused cannot be true?

COMMENTS ON MISCELLANEOUS EXERCISES

1. What can be meant by 'an irrational situation'? A situation is presumably a state of affairs, probably involving people. The implication would seem to be that someone has behaved 'irrationally' (foolishly, inexplicably) in order to bring about this state of affairs. It should certainly be possible to examine and analyse rationally such behaviour and such a situation, though it may be *difficult* to explain it to the general satisfaction.

2. Much to be said for this criticism. But, as we have seen, although it is possible in the closed systems of Geometry and Pure Mathematics to build a set of necessary truths on a solid axiomatic foundation, that is not possible in the shifting, open system of real life.

Nevertheless philosophers and others should obviously make their definitions as clear and unambiguous as possible; absurdity has certainly sometimes resulted from a failure to do this.

3. Two similar but significantly different meanings of 'independence' as applied to opinions:
  i. not dependent on others, forming their own opinions;
  ii. not associated with any particular political party.

Thus a man who after much thought is a convinced socialist has opinions which are independent in the first sense, but not in the other. When one talks about a paper being independent the word is normally used in the second sense; here, rather surprisingly, it is used in the first.

The criticism made was that a paper was more likely to be politically independent if the editor was not committed to a particular party. The 'logical conclusion' would seem to require the following assumptions:

    i. that an editor's strong views on any subject are necessarily reflected in his paper;

    ii. that an objection to the expression of strong views of one kind in one set of circumstances implies an objection to the expression of strong views of all kinds in all circumstances.

4. This is, in a sense, formally correct. We might be prepared to accept the first proposition if what is meant is that those people whom in general we call wise seem on the whole to be happy; and it can be argued that their happiness results from their being wise. But we would not be likely to accept that all wise people are always happy, which is what is stated in the second proposition. 'Wise people' and 'happy people' are not clear-cut groups, and this form of clear-cut argument cannot properly be applied. Most people are happy sometimes and do wise things occasionally.

5. 'Four' is the name for the number that comes after three, that is for three and one. The fact that it is also two and two is implicit in the definitions of the words and can be understood easily by anyone who has grasped these definitions and the idea of number. That is about all the explanation one can give about the meaning of the statement that two and two make four.

'901' is a synonym for '53 times 17' in the sense that they both stand for the same thing, but to say that this is just

like 'violent' being a synonym for 'savage' is misleading
for a variety of reasons.

e.g. i. The 'synonyms' in mathematics are quite precise.
Mr Maugham admits that the synonyms for 'violent' are
not, but seems to imply that the fact that four is a synonym
for three and one as well as for two and two shows a lack
of precision, whereas it merely shows that there are many
synonyms (an indefinitely large number); but each of
them is completely precise.

ii. As a result the meanings of the symbols in mathematics are fixed, whereas the usages of words like
'violent' are variable and subject to change.

iii. The comparison tends to obscure the operations and
manipulations of mathematics which have no counter-
part in the realm of 'violent' and 'savage'.

The point that Mr Maugham probably really had in
mind is that the propositions of mathematics are analytic
and necessary in the same sort of way as the statement of a
definition is analytic and necessary.

6. The first line might be interpreted to mean either (i) that
anyone who rules over freemen (i.e. those who are not
slaves) cannot possibly be a slave himself, or (ii) that in order
to rule effectively over those who are free (perhaps in a
wider sense) one should be free oneself. In either case an
important point is that the relationship between ruling and
being free is such that he who rules is likely to be more free
than those over whom he rules. Is there a similar relationship between driving and being fat? In general, obviously
not. But it might be argued that he who drives fat oxen (and
therefore owns them or is hired by their owner), is likely
himself to be prosperous and therefore fat. But *are* fat oxen
a sign of prosperity or of inefficiency? And why 'should'?

Another possible interpretation is that a fat driver will be sympathetically disposed and less harsh! But even if one accepts either of these, one can hardly agree with Dr Johnson that 'it might as well be said'; the two cases are still not very similar. One might agree warmly with him, however, in not admiring the first line which is very trite and obvious.

7. A cliché is a phrase, usually one that was originally striking and illuminating, often a metaphor, that has become stale by much use and is likely to be employed automatically without thinking about its meaning. 'Cultural heritage' appears to be thought of as a cliché here. 'Humbug' implies sham, deception.

It looks as though the question was not intended to be a genuine one and the cliché is used to assist in making it appear silly or bogus.

8. Mill's arguments for free discussion all amount to saying that it is likely to lead to truer opinions and fuller understanding. This would probably be generally accepted today. But it might be said that in some particular sets of circumstances, for example in war time when there is a danger of spreading alarm and despondency, or when the free discussion leads to slander, there is a case for limiting it. It could be argued that the reasons are still good but they are outweighed by other considerations.

In general it is often true that a principle or a practice which is to the benefit of the community in moderation is not so when pushed to an extreme. Discipline, for example, as applied to the young. Unlimited, undiscriminating generosity would lead to chaos etc.

9. i. seems to have a built-in irrefutability (i.e. it is an *analytic* statement). Whether someone is one of the

'greatest artists' or 'sanest men' would clearly be very much a matter of opinion. But if we did find what appeared to be an exception we could say that history had failed us. Not very clear what the distinction is between 'by the event' and 'by their lives'.

ii. 'Frequently' verifiable in principle, but hardly in practice. Very hard to believe. 'Loosely' a matter of opinion. Perhaps what was meant was: 'The word "freedom" is frequently used; generally very loosely.'

iii. It looks like an analytic statement. How does one decide who has been 'most successful ... etc.'? By seeing whether their 'ideals of human behaviour' are 'singularly alike'?

10. There is explanation by what is usually called mechanical or efficient cause and explanation in terms of purpose, final cause.

11. That the hand reveals a man's nature and fate. The 'must' appears to be logical. The argument is that because a man does things with his hand, and his nature is shown by the sort of things he does, therefore his hand will express his 'innate inherent nature'. Not many people now would think that the premisses justify the conclusion.

12. i. is quoted in J. K. Galbraith's *The Affluent Society*, p. 44. Spencer is saying that, in Galbraith's words, 'to seek to mitigate misery was to put in abeyance the fundamental arrangements by which nature insured progress'. The natural principle, the law of the jungle, must not be interfered with however much suffering it causes.

In ii. Burnham goes on to say that speech cannot be completely free. 'No right guaranteed by any government can, in social fact, be interpreted to permit citizens to advocate, and organize for, mass murder, rape and arson.'

The conflict is between the rigidity of principle and the flexibility of practice. Burnham stresses what the principles are for – organized society. Spencer seems to regard the fundamental law as more important than the improvement of social life, though perhaps he would have said that since what is being proposed breaks this fundamental law it cannot really lead to improvement in the long run.

13. Rational discussion difficult. Words being used rather oddly. It is probably a mystical state that is being described.

14. It does rather look as though the knots here are verbal and the puzzlement home-made. Whether 'intrinsic nature' includes external relations is surely a matter of definition, as is the question whether a patch of colour surrounded by a red ring can be exactly 'like' one that is not. The logical law whereby if a given patch of colour is yellow any patch which is exactly like it is yellow too, is the law which makes any analytic statement true. 'All triangles have three sides' is *necessarily* true, because any figure that didn't have three sides wouldn't count as a triangle. The second patch must be yellow too, because otherwise it wouldn't count as 'exactly alike'. We put the necessity in.

15. Validity of passage clearly dependent on the way in which Descartes handles the concept of perfection; this does not seem to be very consistent or satisfactory. We normally use the adjective 'perfect' in a relative way – related to some purpose. Does it make sense to think of 'Perfection' as an absolute? What would the 'perfect' man be like? Perfectly strong? Perfectly handsome? Perfectly large *and* perfectly small? Perfect for what?

It might be thought that what is superior or more perfect is a matter of opinion. Is it always a 'greater perfection' to know than to doubt? D. sees nothing in earth, light, heat etc. which renders them superior to him. But would he not find heat superior to him for the purpose of warming his dinner? Is it necessary to postulate the existence of a God to explain my idea of someone who can run faster than I can?

16. Descartes could hardly have accepted the second sentence. It couldn't apply to man because no man could be perfect; and it could hardly apply to God, who would then be 'knowing' something that was untrue.

17. Mill's next paragraph runs:

I answer, that it is assuming very much more. There is the greatest difference between presuming an opinion to be true, because, with every opportunity for contesting it, it has not been refuted, and assuming its truth for the purpose of not permitting its refutation. Complete liberty of contradicting and disproving our opinion is the very condition which justifies us in assuming its truth for purposes of action; and on no other terms can a being with human faculties have any rational assurance of being right.

Mill's imaginary opponent is arguing that though we cannot be certain we must act on the best judgement we can form. Mill is arguing that the way which gives, as a general principle, the best chance of the truth being reached, of finding which is the best opinion, is to allow the contrary, and indeed any opinion to be expressed. He might also have pointed out that the analogy of levying taxes or waging war is not a good one and obscures the issue. One could certainly say that just as lack of absolute certainty as to which is the best tax should not prevent a Government from levying any taxes at all, so lack of absolute certainty as to which is the truest opinion should not prevent one from forming or propagating any opinion at all. But beyond this point the analogy breaks down. There is no parallel in the taxation model to the *suppression* of opinions, unless one were to say that just as Governments must prevent others from levying taxes so they must prevent others from propagating opinons. To take it to this point would be to expose the fallacy of argument by analogy. Levying taxes is not much like propagating opinions.

The opponent might merely say that it is to the benefit of society that its members should be protected from perversion by the propagation of false and pernicious opinions. Mill's answer to that would be that any possible gain by suppression would be far outweighed by the loss.

But the peculiar evil of silencing the expression of an opinion is, that it is robbing the human race; posterity as well as the existing generation; those who dissent from the opinion, still more than those who hold it. If the opinion is right, they are deprived of the opportunity of exchanging error for truth: if wrong, they lose, what is almost as great a benefit, the clearer perception and livelier impression of truth, produced by its collision with error. *On Liberty*, p. 79.

18. Bergson goes on to say:

Yes, if we suppose that the arrow can ever *be* in a point of its course. Yes again, if the arrow, which is moving, ever coincides with a position, which is motionless. But the arrow never *is* in any point of its course.

The point, which Bergson goes on to elaborate, is that the paradox rests on a fundamental misunderstanding of the nature of movement.

To suppose that the moving body *is* at a point of its course is to cut the course in two by a snip of the scissors at this point. . . . It is to distinguish two successive acts where, by the hypothesis, there is only one. In short, it is to attribute to the course itself of the arrow everything that can be said of the interval that the arrow has traversed, that is to say, to admit *a priori* the absurdity that movement coincides with immobility.

19. The question as to whether whiteness is a universal is whether it can be said in some sense to exist *apart from* particular white objects, whether in fact 'there are such entities as qualities'. But Russell seems to admit resemblance as a universal simply because there are many instances of things resembling each other.

We shall . . . say that anything is white or a triangle if it has the right sort of resemblance to our chosen particular. But then the resemblance required will have to be a universal. Since there are many white things, the resemblance must hold between many pairs of particular white things; and this is the characteristic of a universal.

One would have thought that in order to admit resemblance as a universal one would have to prove that resemblance exists *apart from* particular cases of things resembling each other. Perhaps however the qualifications for *relations* to be universals are different from those for *qualities*. But in this case it would not seem very logical to use the fact that relations satisfy one set of qualifications as a reason for saying that qualities satisfy another set.

SOURCES OF EXTRACTS

The figures in italic type after each entry indicate the pages in the text on which the extracts are to be found.

ARISTOTLE, *Poetics*. *138*

AUDEN, W. H., *The Dyer's Hand and other Essays*, Faber, 1963. *150*

AUSTIN, J. L., *Sense and Sensibilia*, ed. G. J. Warnock, Oxford University Press, 1962. *59–61, 244*
Philosophical Papers, Oxford University Press, 1961. *66–7*

BELL, CLIVE, *Civilization* (1928); Penguin Books, 1938. *141, 145*

BERGSON, HENRI, *Creative Evolution*, trans. by A. Mitchell, Macmillan, 1911. *67–8, 198, 227, 238, 265–6*

BERKELEY, GEORGE, *Treatise Concerning the Principles of Human Knowledge* (1710); *Three Dialogues between Hylas and Philonous in Opposition to Sceptics and Atheists* (1713); both in *A New Theory of Vision and other Writings*, Dent (Everyman). *51, 156–67, 175–82, 187–8, 194–5*

BERLIN, ISAIAH, *The Age of Enlightenment*, Muller, 1956. (A Mentor Book, New American Library.) *168, 190, 191*
Two Concepts of Liberty, Oxford University Press, 1958. *72*

BOSWELL, JAMES, *The Life of Dr Johnson* (1791), Dent (Everyman) 2 vols. *148, 160, 224, 229–30, 256–7*

BRADLEY, F. H., *Appearance and Reality*, 9th edn, Oxford University Press, 1930. *198*

BRAIN, RUSSELL, *The Humanist Frame* (ed. Julian Huxley, Allen & Unwin, 1961). *185*

BURNHAM, J., *The Struggle for the World*, Cape, 1947. *232, 262*

CARRITT, E. F., *The Theory of Beauty* (5th edn, 1949);
Methuen University Paperbacks, 1962. *138, 139, 231*

CHASE, STUART, *The Power of Words*, Phoenix House, 1955.
45, 54

CHESTERTON, G. K., *Orthodoxy* (1909), Fontana. *226–7*

CONNOLLY, CYRIL, *Enemies of Promise* (1949); Penguin
Books, 1961. *52–3*

CROOKSHANK, F. G., An essay in *The Meaning of Meaning*,
C. K. Ogden and I. A. Richards; Routledge & Kegan Paul,
1923. *68–9*

DESCARTES, RENÉ, *A Discourse on Method* (1637), Dent
(Everyman). *194, 235–6*

DINGLE, H., *The Scientific Adventure*, Pitman, 1952. *161–2, 192*

ELIOT, T. S., *The Function of Criticism* (1923), Faber. *151*

FRANKEL, C., *The Case for Modern Man*, Macmillan, 1957.
224–5, 257

GALBRAITH, J. K., *The Affluent Society*, Hamish Hamilton,
1958. *262*

GELLNER, E., *Words and Things*, Gollancz, 1959. *38*

HARTMAN, R. S., *Value Theory as a Formal System*, Kant-
Studien, Cologne, 1958–9, p. 287. *148–9*

HAYEK, F. A., *The Road to Serfdom*, Routledge, 1946. *83, 245–6*

HEGEL, G. W. F., *The Phenomenology of Mind* (1807), trans.
by J. B. Baillie, 2nd edn, Sonnenschein (Library of Philosophy), 1910. *231–2*

HOBBES, THOMAS, *Leviathan* (1651), Dent (Everyman). *228*

HUME, DAVID, *A Treatise of Human Nature* (1739), Dent
(Everyman), 2 vols. *139–40, 168–73*

HUXLEY, ALDOUS, *Adonis and the Alphabet*, Chatto, 1956. *48*
Brave New World Revisited, Chatto, 1958. *82*
Ends and Means, Chatto, 1937. *231*
The Perennial Philosophy, Chatto, 1946. *236*

JOAD, C. E. M., *Guide to Philosophy*, Gollancz, 1936. *187, 188*

JOSEPH, H. W. B., *Some Problems in Ethics*, Oxford University
Press, 1931. *225–6*

KEYNES, J. M., *The General Theory of Employment, Interest and Money*, Macmillan, 1936. *94–5*

LEAVIS, F. R., *The Common Pursuit*, Chatto, 1952. *80–81, 132, 151*

LEIBNIZ, G. W., *Discourse on Metaphysics*, trans. by P. G. Lucas and L. Grint, Manchester University Press, 1953. *82, 231*

MAUGHAM, W. SOMERSET, *A Writer's Notebook*, Heinemann, 1949. *229*

MILL, JOHN STUART, *On Liberty* (1859), Dent (Everyman). *230, 236–7, 264, 265*
A System of Logic (1843), (Sir John Lubbock's Hundred Books.) *58, 243–4*

MOORE, G. E., *Philosophical Studies* (1922), Routledge, paperback, 1960. *65–6, 148, 195–6, 233–5*
Principia Ethica (1903), Cambridge University Press, paperback, 1960. *139, 140–41*

MORGAN, CHARLES, *Liberties of the Mind*, Macmillan, 1951. *31, 233*

ORWELL, GEORGE, *Nineteen Eighty-four* (1949), Penguin Books, 1954. *55–6*

PLATO, *The Republic*, trans. by F. Cornford, Oxford University Press, 1941. *138*; trans. by H. D. P. Lee, Penguin Books, 1955. *196–8*
The Symposium, trans. by W. Hamilton, Penguin Books, 1951. *138*

POPPER, K. R., *The Logic of Scientific Discovery*, Hutchinson, 1956. *20*

REID, L. A., *Philosophy and Education*, Heinemann, 1962. *100*

RUSSELL, BERTRAND, *History of Western Philosophy*, Allen & Unwin, 1946. *48, 173*
The Problems of Philosophy, Oxford University Press (Home University Library), 1912. *154–6, 238–9, 266*
Wisdom of the West, Macdonald, 1959. *17*

RYLE, GILBERT, *The Concept of Mind*, Hutchinson (University Library), 1949. *59, 71–2, 95*

SHELLEY, P. B., *A Defence of Poetry. Prose Works* (ed. H. Buxton Forman, 1880). *195*

SIDGWICK, HENRY, *Methods of Ethics* (1874), Macmillan, 1963. *141*

SPENCER, HERBERT, *Essays on Education* (1861), Dent (Everyman). *83–4*
Principles of Ethics (New York, Appleton, 1897.) *232*

TOMLIN, E. W. F., *Great Philosophers of the West* (1950), Hutchinson (Grey Arrow), 1959. *19, 188*

WARNOCK, G. J., *English Philosophy since 1900*. Oxford University Press (Home University Library), 1958. *38–9*

WHITEHEAD, A. N., *Adventures of Ideas* (1933), Penguin Books, 1942. *18, 57–8*

WITTGENSTEIN, L. J. J., *Philosophical Investigations*, trans. by G. E. M. Anscombe, Blackwell, 1953. *18, 56–7, 108*

WODEHOUSE, P. G., *The Man with Two Left Feet*, Penguin Books, 1961. *144*

YOUNG, J. Z., *Doubt and Certainty in Science* (Reith Lectures, 1950), Oxford University Press, 1951. *36–7, 69–70, 198*

FOR THE BEST IN PAPERBACKS, LOOK FOR THE 🐧

In every corner of the world, on every subject under the sun, Penguin represents quality and variety – the very best in publishing today.

For complete information about books available from Penguin – including Puffins, Penguin Classics and Arkana – and how to order them, write to us at the appropriate address below. Please note that for copyright reasons the selection of books varies from country to country.

In the United Kingdom: Please write to *Dept E.P., Penguin Books Ltd, Harmondsworth, Middlesex, UB7 0DA.*

If you have any difficulty in obtaining a title, please send your order with the correct money, plus ten per cent for postage and packaging, to *PO Box No 11, West Drayton, Middlesex*

In the United States: Please write to *Dept BA, Penguin, 299 Murray Hill Parkway, East Rutherford, New Jersey 07073*

In Canada: Please write to *Penguin Books Canada Ltd, 2801 John Street, Markham, Ontario L3R 1B4*

In Australia: Please write to the *Marketing Department, Penguin Books Australia Ltd, P.O. Box 257, Ringwood, Victoria 3134*

In New Zealand: Please write to the *Marketing Department, Penguin Books (NZ) Ltd, Private Bag, Takapuna, Auckland 9*

In India: Please write to *Penguin Overseas Ltd, 706 Eros Apartments, 56 Nehru Place, New Delhi, 110019*

In the Netherlands: Please write to *Penguin Books Netherlands B.V., Postbus 195, NL–1380AD Weesp*

In West Germany: Please write to *Penguin Books Ltd, Friedrichstrasse 10–12, D–6000 Frankfurt/Main 1*

In Spain: Please write to *Longman Penguin España, Calle San Nicolas 15, E–28013 Madrid*

In Italy: Please write to *Penguin Italia s.r.l., Via Como 4, I-20096 Pioltello (Milano)*

In France: Please write to *Penguin Books Ltd, 39 Rue de Montmorency, F-75003 Paris*

In Japan: Please write to *Longman Penguin Japan Co Ltd, Yamaguchi Building, 2–12–9 Kanda Jimbocho, Chiyoda-Ku, Tokyo 101*